THE HIDDEN LIFE OF THE
ANCIENT
MAYA

THE HIDDEN LIFE OF THE
ANCIENT MAYA

REVELATIONS FROM A MYSTERIOUS WORLD

CLARE GIBSON

METRO BOOKS
NEW YORK

This 2010 edition published by Metro Books,
by arrangement with Saraband.

Edited by Sara Hunt
Design by Deborah White

Metro Books
122 Fifth Avenue
New York, NY 10011

ISBN-13: 978-1-4351-2697-8

Printed and bound in China

1 3 5 7 9 10 8 6 4 2

Page 2: *Detail of a Late Classic mural at the Painted Temple of Bonampak, depicting musicians playing drums, turtle carapaces, rattles and trumpets (see pages 180 to 183).*

Page 3: *Detail of a Maya warrior with spear and shield, from a Late Classic cylindrical earthenware vessel (see pages 168 to 173).*

For John and Marianne Gibson

CONTENTS

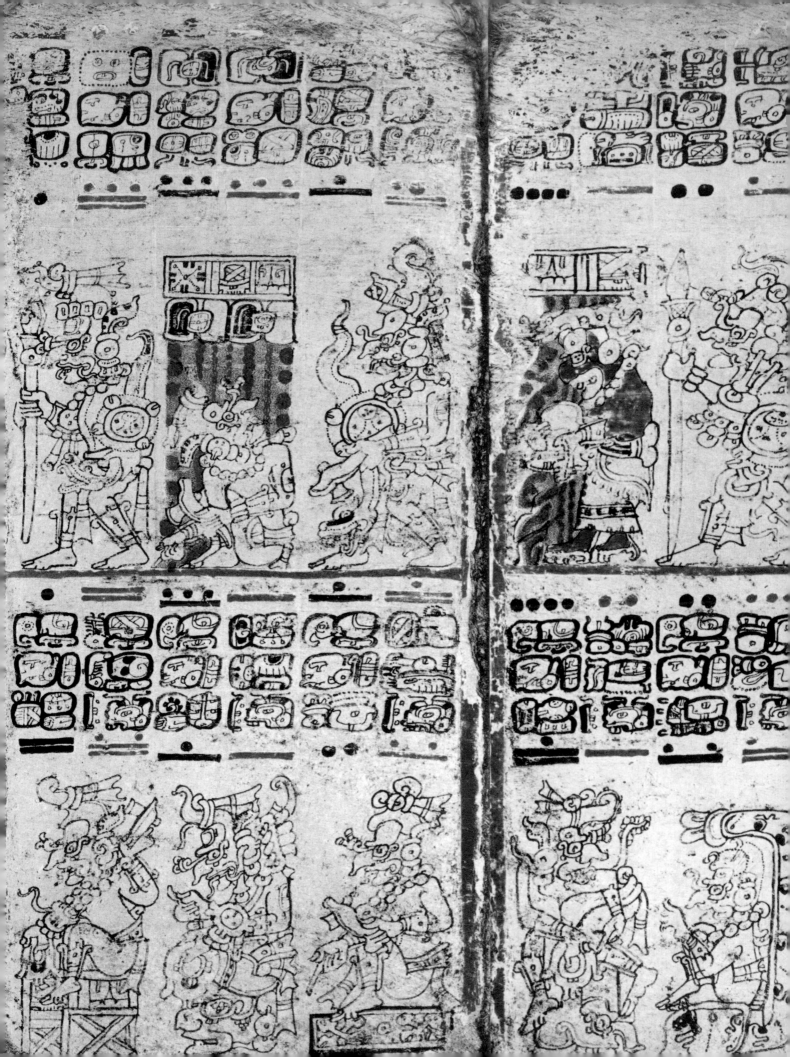

FOREWORD

*Thus they caused the face of the earth to
be darkened, and there fell a black rain, a
rain that fell both night and day. The small
and the great animals came in upon them.
Their faces were crushed by the trees and the
stones. They were spoken to by all their maize
grinders and their cooking griddles, their
plates and their pots, their dogs and their
grinding stones. However many things they
had, all of them crushed their faces.*
*… Thus the framed people, the shaped people,
were undone. They were demolished and
overthrown as people. The mouths and the faces
of all of them were crushed and ruined.*

—"The Fall of the Effigies of Carved Wood,"
Popol Vuh: The Sacred Book of the Maya,
translated by Allen J. Christenson, 2003.

Above: *The pronounced headgear and oversized earrings
on this figure signify the person's high social status.*
Opposite: *Pages from the Förstemann version of the Dresden
Codex, an invaluable document dating from the sixteenth
century that has greatly aided our understanding of the Maya
way of life.*

Will the world as we know it end on December 21 (or 23), 2012? It seems unlikely to those of us who remember the doom-laden predictions that preceded the dawning of the second millennium, none of which came to pass when the year 1999 actually gave way to 2000. Humankind has an innate tendency to see coincidences as omens, and it so happens that two events (which may, or may not, be coincidental) will occur across time and space on December 21, 2012: it will be the winter solstice, the shortest day of the year; and the Maya Long Count, a 5125-year-long calendrical cycle measuring out an age that began on August 11 (or 13), 3114 BC, will come to an end.

And not only are we humans prone to regarding omens as portents of disaster, but we also like to imbue certain numbers with symbolic significance. The number 13, for instance, is considered unlucky in the Christianized West because thirteen people were present at the Last Supper that preceded Christ's crucifixion, while 0's representation of nothingness is negatively reflected in the terms "zero hour" and "ground zero," which respectively refer to the moment when a critical event is scheduled to occur and the area marking the central point of a nuclear explosion

or catastrophic occurrence. Viewed in this dark light, the ancient Maya identifier for the date that we call December 21, 2012—13.0.0.0.0—appears chillingly ominous. When one then factors in the accuracy, complexity, and prophetic purpose of the ancient Maya people's systems of astronomical observation, their intricately written and illustrated records, as well as the mysterious decline of their impressively advanced civilization at a time when Europe was living in the so-called "Dark Ages," it is, perhaps, not surprising that all manner of "end-time" scenarios have been envisaged for December 21, 2012.

According to the "galactic alignment" theory, for instance, the positions of the sun and Earth on the galactic plane will be in exact alignment with the Dark Rift, an area comprising dust clouds near the heart of the Milky Way Galaxy. The Maya association of the Dark Rift with the *xibalba be*, the "black road" to the underworld, may furthermore have inspired the idea that our planet will be swallowed up by Sagittarius A*, a supermassive black hole at the center of the Milky Way, on 13.0.0.0.0. Alternatively, the Earth may be obliterated following a collision with a mythical planet named either Nibiru or Planet X, or else Eris, an actual dwarf planet, or perhaps an asteroid. Or maybe a solar maximum (increased solar activity, that is, solar flares, coronal mass ejections, and sunspots) will trigger a polar shift or geomagnetic reversal of the Earth's north and south magnetic poles, exposing us, and our computer systems, to all manner of perilous cosmic influences. Other

Left: *The impressive pyramids at Tikal, in northern Guatemala, which was the capital of a conquest state that became one of the most powerful kingdoms of the ancient Maya during the Classic period, c. 250–900.*

Long Count is currently charting will then run its course, and that its termination will prompt the start of a new age, and of a new "great cycle," or Long Count.

Although far less is known about the civilization constructed by the ancient Maya than, for example, that of ancient Egypt, the past decades have seen a significant increase in our understanding of their remarkable culture, thanks both to new discoveries and to the advances made by a dedicated community of Mayanists. As a result, the texts spelled out by Maya glyphs are no longer so mysterious, and the intricate workings of the Maya calendars—including the Long Count—are far better understood. Many an excitable imagination has since been fired up by the prospect of the Long Count's end, fueled, for example, by cataclysmic passages from interpretations of the Quiché Maya's sacred book, the *Popol Vuh*. The following extract, for instance, describes the terrible destruction that ended the age of the people made of wood and reeds, which followed those of the creation of the earth and mountains, the animals, and the mud person, and which preceded the creation of humankind:

> *Then came the end of the effigies carved of wood, for they were ruined, crushed, and killed. A flood was planned by Heart of Sky that came down upon the heads of the effigies carved of wood.*
>
> *The body of man had been carved of tz'ite wood by the Framer and the Shaper. The body of woman consisted of reeds according to the desire of the Framer and the Shaper. But they were not capable of understanding and did not speak before their Framer and their Shaper, their makers and their creators.*
>
> *Thus they were killed in the flood. There came a great resin down from the sky."*

suggestions are less apocalyptic, however, focusing as they do on the dawning of a new global consciousness. Yet once the speculation surrounding the possibly cataclysmic events set in motion by the arrival of December 21, 2012 are set aside, the only two remaining certainties are that this date marks the winter solstice and the end of the Long Count. But if, as some believe, 13.0.0.0.0 equates to December 23, 2012, then all that we can confidently conclude is that the era that the

This catastrophe has striking parallels with the great flood that is familiar to us from the Old Testament and other traditions, and is therefore seen by some as proof of the Maya civilization's apparently mystical knowledge of the past, present, and future. Those who have devoted themselves to studying the ancient Maya, however, have felt obliged to explain that there is simply no evidence that the Maya themselves would have considered the arrival of the Long Count's end date of 13.0.0.0.0 as anything more significant than a cause for festivity, and that a new cycle would then have followed—just as we celebrate the New Year as December 31 gives way to January 1 before returning to business as usual on January 2. Indeed, the ancient Maya literally set dates later than 13.0.0.0.0 in stone, a prediction, for instance, having been carved in the seventh century, on a monument in the city of Palenque's Temple of Inscriptions, stating that the eightieth calendar-round anniversary of King Pacal's coronation would be marked on October 15, 4772.

Those Mayanists (and twenty-first-century astronomers) who found themselves repeatedly explaining that the evidence—historical, as well as scientific—points overwhelmingly against the

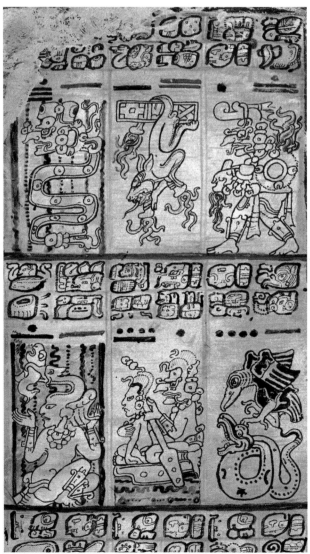

Left, above and opposite: Pages from the colorful Kingsborough (left) and Förstemann (above) versions of the Dresden Codex and the Madrid Codex (opposite).

ancient Maya having foreseen the demise of the world in December 2012 have therefore had their patience sorely tried in recent years. Nevertheless, it cannot be denied that the age of the dinosaurs was at least hastened, and possibly even terminated, by an asteroid strike; that life-obliterating ice ages have literally changed the face of the world in the past; and that the Maya civilization is just one example of a spectacularly successful society that experienced a sudden and disastrous decline for reasons that are not entirely clear to us. And no one can dismiss the terrible dangers that threaten our planet in the form of potentially catastrophic climate change, volcanic eruptions, tsunamis, and earthquakes, or,

in an unstable world that contains rogue states and fanatical terrorists, nuclear and biological warfare and other manmade horrors. So maybe it is not so far-fetched to imagine that the age of humankind could be destroyed as conclusively as that of the people made of wood and reeds, as related in the *Popol Vuh*. On a more positive note, the increased general interest in the Maya triggered by the countdown to the completion of the Long Count should be welcomed. For it has opened many people's eyes to the rich culture of the ancient Maya as expressed through the breathtaking art, artifacts, and architecture that have survived as testimony to their creators' sophistication and skill.

INTRODUCTION

Before the Spaniards subdued the country the Indians lived together in well ordered communities; they kept the ground in excellent condition, free from noxious vegetation and planted with fine trees. The habitation was as follows: in the center of town were the temples, with beautiful plazas, and around the temples stood the houses of the chiefs and the priests, and next those of the leading men. Closest to these came the houses of those who were wealthiest and most esteemed, and at the borders of the town were the houses of the common people. The wells, where they were few, were near the houses of the chiefs; their plantations were set out in the trees for making wine, and sown with cotton, pepper and maize. They lived in these communities for fear of their enemies, lest they be taken in captivity; but after the wars with the Spaniards they dispersed through the forests.

—Diego de Landa, *Relación de las Cosas de Yucatán*, 1566 (*Yucatán Before and After the Conquest*, translation by William Gates).

Above: *Stela D, at Copán, portrays King Eighteen Rabbit, who was captured and killed in AD 738, two years after this monument was raised.*
Opposite: *Sculpted images of Kukulcan, the Feathered Serpent, are positioned at the top of Chichén Itzá's Temple of the Warriors.*

Writing not long after the Spanish conquest of the Yucatán Peninsula began, the Spanish cleric Diego de Landa (1524–79) described in his eye-witness narrative the communities that the indigenous people of this Maya region had lived in before the arrival of the European invaders. Despite regarding it through "Old World," devout Roman Catholic eyes, de Landa found much to commend in the land of a people whose vices he disapprovingly listed as being "idolatry, divorce, public orgies, and the buying and selling of slaves." Indeed, interspersed with tales of "their superstitions and deceits" and "filthy and grievous sacrifice," he wonderingly speaks of "many edifices of great beauty," as well as of the principal lords learning "from interest, and for the greater esteem they enjoyed thereby ..."

Nearly three centuries after de Landa's account, the US explorer John Lloyd Stephens (1805–52) noted in his book *Incidents of Travel in Central America, Chiapas and Yucatán* (1841) that discovering an altar amid the ruins of Copán, in the company of British architect Frederick Catherwood (1799–1854), "gave us the assurance that the objects we were in search of were interesting, not only as the remains of an unknown people, but as works of art, proving, like newly-discovered historical records, that the people who once occupied the Continent of America were not savages." Indeed they were not.

It is now well over a hundred and fifty years since Stephens and Catherwood rediscovered Copán, Palenque, and other long-abandoned Mesoamerican sites and cities, and during that time scholars have uncovered and learned an astonishing amount of amazing information about the people who constructed them: the ancient Maya.

The Rise and Fall of the Ancient Maya

We now know that the ancient Maya rose to prominence in a Central American area roughly equivalent to southeastern Mexico in the west, through the Yucatán Peninsula, Guatemala, Belize, and northwestern Honduras to northwestern El Salvador in the east. Well established by the time of what is known as the Formative, or Preclassic, Period (2000 BC–AD 250), the civilization presided over by the ancient Maya flourished during the Classic Period (AD 250–900), the Postclassic Period (AD 900–1521), however, marking a steady decline that the Spanish Conquest, initiated in the land of the Aztecs by conquistador Hernán Cortés (1485–1547), finally terminated. No one knows exactly why such a sophisticated and successful civilization should apparently have been failing for some time before the Old World was infiltrated by the New, but catastrophic climate change—specifically drought—agricultural failure, and endemic warfare have all been proposed as triggers for its ultimate collapse.

The Spanish may have done their best to obliterate as much of the ancient Maya culture that they considered "idolatrous" as they could, and other circumstances may also have been against them, but the Maya people themselves survived, today being thought to number around 6 million. And the inherited customs and traditions of the modern Maya continue to give Mayanists (as the scholars who

---

ANCIENT MAYA TIMELINE

Sources vary as to dates; some Mayanists also refer to a Terminal Classic Period within the Late Classic dates given here, c.650–900.

Formative/Preclassic Period 2000 BC–AD 250
Early Formative/Preclassic Period 2000–900 BC
Middle Formative/Preclassic Period 900–400 BC
Late Formative/Preclassic Period 400 BC–AD 250

Classic Period AD 250–900
Early Classic Period 250–550
Late Classic Period 550–900

Postclassic Period AD 900–1521
Early Postclassic Period 900–1200
Late Postclassic Period 1200–1521

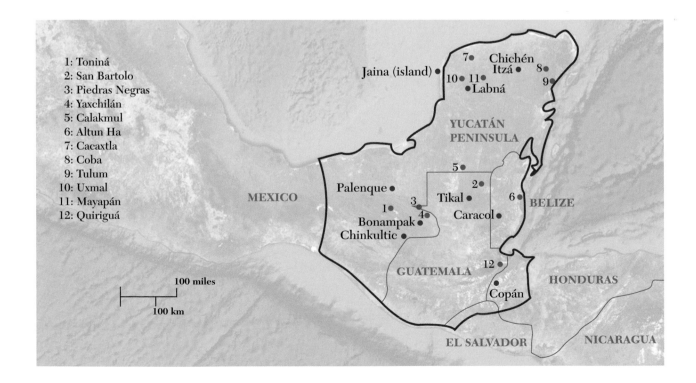

1: Toniná
2: San Bartolo
3: Piedras Negras
4: Yaxchilán
5: Calakmul
6: Altun Ha
7: Cacaxtla
8: Coba
9: Tulum
10: Uxmal
11: Mayapán
12: Quiriguá

100 miles
100 km

Right: *An Olmec terra-cotta "baby-face" figure. The civilization founded by the ancient Olmec is regarded as being Mesoamerica's first.*
Opposite: *A map showing the extent of the ancient Maya civilization and its major sites.*

specialize in studying the ancient Maya are collectively called) intriguing insights into the minds, myths, and motives of their ancestors, just as historical records like de Landa's have proved invaluable in painting a picture of a long-lost world of pre-Columbian places and peoples.

Art and Architecture

In recent decades, the painstaking work of Mayanists from all manner of disciplines—including archeologists, historians and scientists, artists and photographers, epigraphers and linguists—helped by some significant intellectual breakthroughs and technical advances, have contributed immensely to our knowledge of the lives and times of the ancient Maya.

Rather than being a peaceful, agrarian people, as was once thought, there is today no doubt that the Maya—who were never a unified political or national entity, instead comprising around sixty city-states—waged vigorous war against each other, city against city, led by the kings and warlords who stood at the top of the social pyramid. And although they cultivated maize, cacao, and other agricultural products for sustenance, made ceramics, and wove their own cotton cloth, they also imported and exported a wide variety of goods through important trading networks. Nor did the ancient Maya exist in a cultural vacuum, for not only were they the inheri-

tors of the legacy left by the earlier Olmec, but they were open to influence from their neighbors, too, as is evident, for example, in the Toltec-inspired architectural features discernible at the still spectacular, albeit deserted, Maya city of Chichén Itzá (see pages 18 to 31).

As de Landa observed in 1566, the Maya cities of Yucatán and elsewhere were something to behold, even in their abandoned state:

> *If the number, grandeur and beauty of its buildings were to count toward the attainment of renown and reputation in the same way as gold, silver and riches have done for other parts of the Indies, Yucatan would have become as famous as Peru and New Spain have become, so many, in so many places, and so well built of stone are they, it is a marvel; the buildings themselves, and their number, are the most outstanding thing that has been discovered in the Indies.*

They may not be able to compete with pyramid-temples like Chichén Itzá's "Castillo" for sheer size, but much of the art and artifacts created by ancient Maya artists and craftsmen are equally impressive in their own smaller way, be they intricately carved

stelae or lintels, skillfully painted cylinder vessels and murals, unnervingly lifelike figures from Jaina, striking-looking incensarios, or any of the other objects that advertise Maya artistry, a number of which are featured within this book.

Cosmic Connections

Among the most astounding of the Maya achievements—and just how astounding is only now becoming clear—were, perhaps, those that lay in the realm of the abstract: in the Maya ability, through astronomical observations, to track the past, present, and future through the development and use of the 260-day calendar (the *tzolkin*), the 365-day calendar (the *haab*), and the Long Count (the 5125-year count, whose current cycle is due to end in December 2012). As de Landa observed: "With these periodical returns and the complicated count, it is a marvel to see the freedom with which they know how to count and understand things."

And it is primarily through the work carried out by epigraphers in decoding Maya hieroglyphs, or glyphs—the complex form of writing with which the Maya recorded significant dates and other concepts by incising them on stone monuments, painting them on ceramic vessels, and inscribing them in the illustrated codices, or books (of which only four have survived the Spanish Maya-book-burning frenzy)—that our previously narrow perspective on the Maya world has been opened up and widened to cosmic levels.

Supported by the story related in the *Popol Vuh* (the creation account of the Quiché Maya, of the southern Guatemalan highlands, which is believed to have been set down during the 1550s), and given visual expression in, for example, a symbolically related Mesoamerican artifact, the Aztec Sun Stone (see pages 198 to 201), it has become clear that the Maya had a sophisticated view of time and the universe, and of their place within

Right: The Pyramid of the Magician at Uxmal, in northwest Yucatán, is notable for having been constructed on an oval-shaped base.
Opposite: The ruined "El Castillo" (Spanish for "The Castle," but actually a pyramid) at Xunantunich, Belize.
Below: Dating from 1566, Diego de Landa's Relación de las Cosas de Yucatán (An Account of the Things of Yucatán/Yucatán Before and After the Conquest) *is an important source of information for Mayanists. Reproduced below is a page from the original manuscript showing de Landa's illustrations of some Maya glyphs, which he wrongly describes as the "a, b, c" of the "Indians."*

both, seeing cosmic connections everywhere. They believed that their gods had not only created them, but enabled their continuing survival, and that it was consequently their duty to commune with, honor, and sustain the deities through offerings and sacrifice (including bloodletting and human sacrifice), as well as through the punctilious performance of sacred rituals and ceremonies, be they on a ballcourt or high on the summit of a pyramid. Divine influence affected every aspect of their everyday lives, they believed, and failure to propitiate perhaps the rain god Chac correctly, or to manage the malign influence of the planet Venus, could result in catastrophe. And when their life on earth was over, the Maya expected to journey elsewhere within the cosmos: first, to the underworld (which they called *xibalba*), and then, if they survived this "place of fright," to follow in the footsteps of the Maize God, ultimately to the heavenly realms.

Just as death was not considered the end for the ancient Maya, nor have their cultural achievements been extinguished, experiencing as these are an exhilarating rebirth, thanks to those who have been inspired by the wisdom of the ancient Maya to learn more. Over five hundred years since it faded into the shadows of history, the hidden life of the ancient Maya is at last again being revealed in all of its colorful glory.

Maya or Mayan?

When referring to the Maya and their world, Mayanists have agreed to use "Maya" as both a noun and an adjective (for instance, "the Maya people," or the "Maya calendar), reserving "Mayan" for the Mayan language and related adjectives ("the Mayan word *cauac*," for instance).

SET IN STONE

Decoding a Maya Site: Chichén Itzá

The opinion of the Indians is that with the Itzás who settled Chichén Itzá there ruled a great lord named Culculcán [Kukulcan], as an evidence of which the principal building is called Culculcán. They say that he came from the West, but are not agreed as to whether he came before or after the Itzás, or with them. They say that he was well disposed, that he had no wife or children, and that after his return he was regarded in Mexico as one of their gods, and called Cezalcohuati [Quetzalcoatl].

—Diego de Landa, *Relación de las Cosas de Yucatán*, 1566 (*Yucatán Before and After the Conquest*, translation by William Gates).

*C*hichén Itzá has been translated as "Opening of the Wells of the Itzá," the name of this Maya site referring to the two cenotes (sinkholes) that, in the absence of other freshwater sources, must initially have attracted settlers to this northerly spot in the Yucatán Peninsula. And although scholars remain uncertain regarding the exact dates and sequence of events, it seems that Chichén Itzá was already well established by the tenth century AD, when a surge in Toltec influence from Central Mexico caused it to become the most powerful Maya city in the region, its success being primarily built on the twin planks of coastal trade and warfare. Its supremacy in Yucatán lasted for around two centuries, the terminal decline that Chichén Itzá entered in about 1200 being confirmed when it was eclipsed by the city of Mayapán, which became pre-eminent toward the end of the thirteenth century. Despite its plummeting fortunes, Chichén Itzá retained a notable asset, however: the Sacred Cenote (or Well of Sacrifice), one of the

Opposite: This view of the ranks of columns outside the Temple of the Warriors dramatically illustrates the types of colonnades that the Toltec influence introduced to Maya architecture.

two *cenotes* that had drawn the Maya to it in the first place, which remained the focus of pilgrimages by the people of Yucatán. Nevertheless, as the Spanish bishop Diego de Landa reported following his visit to Chichén Itzá during the sixteenth century: "The building and the sites, both beautiful, and only ten leagues from the sea, with fertile fields and districts all about, were deserted."

A Maya–Toltec Fusion

While the archeological evidence leaves no doubt that the existing Maya city of Chichén Itzá was significantly shaped by Toltec-inspired influences from around the tenth century, it is not certain whether these were imposed by conquest or were peacefully assimilated through, for example, trading links. A number of tales survive that tell of the arrival in 987 from the Central Mexican city of Tollán (or Tula) of a Toltec figure who was part culture hero and part deity, and who inaugurated a golden age in Chichén Itzá. This was Ce Acatl Topiltzin Quetzalcoatl, whom legend equates with the god Quetzalcoatl, or, as the Maya called this "Feathered Serpent" deity, Kukulcan.

Whatever the true circumstances behind the adoption of elements of Toltec style in Chichén Itzá, a clear division between the site's pre- and post-Toltec period is evident in its architecture. In the south, the earlier part of Chichén Itzá, the traditional Maya Puuc style of the Late Classic Period prevails, while in the north, architectural features reveal a Central Mexican preoccupation with the Feathered Serpent, as well as with warriorship and human sacrifice, that shared much with Toltec Tollán.

The style named for the Puuc Hills of Yucatán and Campeche is characterized by unadorned lower walls, with the upper façades being decorated with friezes filled with repetitive, latticelike patterns and columns, and sometimes also with deity masks. Many of these characteristics can be seen at Chichén Itzá, including in the "Nunnery" (also known as the Casa de las Monjas), which also incorporates elements of the elaborate Chenes style that flourished in the Yucatán Peninsula during the Late Classic Period; the Red House (or Casa Colorada or Chichan-Chob); the Akabdzib (or Hidden Writing House); the House of Deer; and the Caracol (or Observatory).

In many respects less abstract than the Puuc style, the Postclassic Period Toltec influence on Chichén Itzá's architecture is especially evident in the colonnades seen in the northern section of the site, for instance, at the Hall of the Thousand Columns. Other Toltec-inspired details are the chacmool figures of reclining men that may have served to hold the hearts of human sacrificial victims; the standing "Atlantean figures" that were designed to support such structures as lintels; the seated standard-bearer figures that once held banners; and the stone replica of the *tzompantli*, or wooden skull rack.

Chichén Itzá's Cosmic Layout

Many of the ceremonial centers of Maya cities conformed to a layout that was carefully planned to mirror the form that the cosmos was envisaged as taking, with the north being believed to approach the heavens, and the south being thought of as pointing toward the underworld, with east being significant as the direction in which the sun rises at dawn, and west, where it sets at dusk (see also pages 42 to 46). In addition, certain sacred buildings were specifically associated with the heavens

Opposite: A mask has been positioned at the center of a section of the Caracol's tower where the Puuc-style decoration is still evident.
Below: A figure wearing a feathered headdress has been portrayed on the façade of a wing of the Puuc-style building known as the "Nunnery."

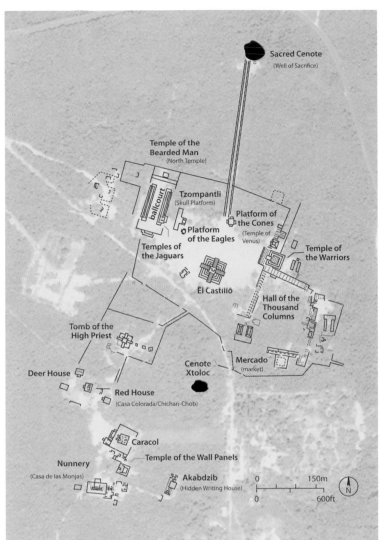

sacbé linking this northern group of buildings with the Caracol.

Included amid the northern, Toltec-style monuments, and constructed from west to east, are the Great Ballcourt, the Upper and Lower Temples of the Jaguars, the Platform of the Eagles, the *tzompantli*, the Platform of the Cones (or Temple of Venus), and the "Castillo." Farther east lies the Temple of the Warriors, the Hall of the Thousand Columns, and the Mercado (or Market), with the building known as the High Priest's Tomb being positioned to the south of the Great Ballcourt, and the Red House to the south of that. The Caracol is situated to the southeast of the Red House, with other, earlier, Puuc-style structures lying farther to the south, including the Temple of the Wall Panels and the "Nunnery."

While many elements are common to other Maya cities, too—notably a plaza (which symbolized a sacred lake or primordial waters), a great pyramidal temple (representing a sacred mountain), a ballcourt (signifying a sacred cavern), and sacred ways, unlike at Palenque, for example, there seems to be no grand palace at Chichén Itzá. This apparent absence may reflect the city's lack of divine king (it is thought that it was instead ruled by a council of the élite).

The Sacred Cenote
Writing in his eye-witness narrative *Relación de las Cosas de Yucatán* (*An Account of the Things in Yucatán*, or *Yucatán Before and After the Conquest*) in 1566, Diego de Landa described the *sacbé* leading to the Sacred Cenote as a "beautiful broad paved way," and the cenote itself as being "seven long fathoms deep to the surface of the water, more than a hundred feet wide, round, of natural rock marvelously

(temples atop pyramids, for instance), with others, such as ballcourts and cenotes, being considered to be entrances to the underworld (which the Maya called *xibalba*, or "place of fright").

Chichén Itzá's plan is roughly oriented from north-north-east to south-south-west, with the Sacred Cenote being positioned in the far north. (The city's other natural sinkhole, the Cenote Xtoloc, which provided inhabitants with water, lies to the east of the Red House and to the south of the "Castillo," or Temple of Kukulcan.) As at other Maya ceremonial centers, a sacred way or causeway—a raised stone road with a white-plastered surface called a *sacbé* (or *sak beh*, "white way")—connects disparate sacred features and elements at Chichén Itzá, with a *sacbé* linking the Sacred Cenote with the plaza within which the "Castillo" is situated, and another

smooth down to the water. The water looks green, caused as I think by the trees that surround it; it is very deep." Created naturally through the collapse of porous limestone rock to expose the pooled rainwater below, this particular sinkhole was 70 ft (21 m) deep. Like other sinkholes in the Yucatán Peninsula, it was considered sacred to Chac, the Maya god of rain, water, thunder, and lightning (see also pages 102 to 105), and, as its alternative name, the Well of Sacrifice, suggests, it consequently acted as a receptacle for sacrificial offerings ritually dedicated to this deity, as related by de Landa: "Into this well they were and still are accustomed to throw men alive as a sacrifice to the gods in times of drought; they held that they did not die, even though they were not seen again. They also threw in many other offerings of precious stones and things they valued greatly…" Indeed, human bones, as well as such valuable votive offerings as jade plaques have been recovered from the depths of the Sacred Cenote, offering valuable insights into Maya ritual practices, as well as Maya artifacts.

The Great Ballcourt and the *Tzompantli*

The Great Ballcourt lies within the plaza, to the southwest of the Sacred Cenote. The biggest of the thirteen ballcourts believed to have been at Chichén Itzá—and, in fact, the largest anywhere in Mesoamerica—the "I"-shaped Great Ballcourt has steep vertical side walls, with low, sloping benches running along the sides, and low end walls. Positioned high up in the middle of each side wall is a hooped stone circle through which players vied to pass the heavy rubber ball, if not in actual practice, then in theory, for the Great Ballcourt may well have served a purely ritual function in recreating or celebrating the victory of the Hero Twins over the death lords of *xibalba* on an underworld ballcourt, as related in the Quiché Maya's sacred text, the *Popol Vuh* (see pages 47 to 49).

The six bas-relief scenes incised on panels decorating the sides (three per side) have provided Mayanists with some important information about how the ballgame was played, or envisaged, at Chichén Itzá: with seven players per side, and as a matter of life and death, for the losers were seemingly decapitated. This practice explains the presence of the *tzompantli*, or the stone platform alongside the Great Ballcourt that, with its depiction around the sides of tiered skulls impaled on poles, replicates the wooden skull racks that once displayed the skulls of those who had been ritually sacrificed to the gods through beheading. Indeed, it is thought that the platform itself probably supported such skull racks. Although the Maya had

Top: The deep, green water of the Sacred Cenote. It is easy to see why this natural well was accorded such significance.
Left: Decorated with an undulating serpentine pattern, this stone ring was attached to one of the Great Ballcourt's side walls at a height of around 26 ft (8 m). The aim was for ballplayers to pass the ball through the ring.

Opposite above: A stone-ring "goal" and the Upper Temple of the Jaguars are visible in this view of the Great Ballcourt's eastern side wall from the ballgame-playing area.
Opposite below: Rows of skulls impaled upon stakes have been portrayed around the sides of the stone tzompantli platform adjacent to the Great Ballcourt.

long practiced human sacrifice—and the *Popol Vuh* furthermore refers to Hun Hunahpuh's head being placed in a symbolically related roadside calabash tree, while his body was buried beneath Crushing Ballcourt in *xibalba*—the *tzompantli* is considered by scholars to be more a feature of Toltec architecture than of Maya.

Stairways on the outer sides of the ballcourt's walls lead to the top, where six small structures once stood (three atop each wall). The largest, on the eastern wall, survives, this being the Upper Temple of the Jaguars, whose interior walls are

decorated with painted murals depicting battle scenes of significance to Chichén Itzá's history or mythology. Below the Upper Temple of the Jaguars is the Lower Temple of the Jaguars, where there is a stone jaguar throne. And at the center of the northern end wall stands the North Temple (which is also known as the Temple of the Bearded Man), on whose exterior balustrades can be seen sculpted World Tree images (see pages 42 to 46), and whose interior walls display richly illustrated bas-relief scenes, among them some relating to the ritual aspects of the ballgame.

The Temple of the Warriors and *Chacmools*

On the opposite, eastern side of the plaza to the Great Ballcourt stands the Temple of the Warriors, a square, four-level pyramidal construction at the top of which, reached by a central stairway, is the temple's sanctuary. Dedicated, it is thought, to Kukulcan in his aspect of Venus, the "Morning Star," and, in this form, a deity especially associated with war (see pages 64 to 66), the Temple of the Warriors is not only positioned close to the Platform of the Cones (or Temple of Venus), where rituals honoring Venus were performed, but also supports clear examples of martial imagery. The ranks of square columns at the base of the pyramid, for instance, have been adorned with carvings portraying warriors (and it is they that give the temple its name). (Another stone colonnade, that of the now roofless hypostyle Hall of the Thousand Columns, which may once have been used as a meeting place, runs adjacent to the Temple of the Warriors.) And bas-relief panels include images of jaguars and eagles—creatures after which two warrior orders were named at Chichén Itzá—devouring hearts.

At the top of the stairway, in front of the Temple of the Warriors' sanctuary, stands a *chacmool*, a sculptural Toltec innovation to Maya sacred art that takes the form of a male figure (maybe a cap-

Left: Also known as the Temple of the Bearded Man, the North Temple is situated at the northern end of the Great Ballcourt and displays extraordinarily detailed bas-relief scenes on its interior walls.
Opposite: A stone jaguar throne, flanked by two columns, stands at the entrance to the Lower Temple of the Jaguars.

tive or fallen warrior) sculpted in stone, and seen in profile apparently sitting on the ground, with his knees bent, leaning back a little on his elbows as he turns his head to an angle of 90 degrees to stare at the viewer. His hands hold a bowl positioned in the angle formed between his thighs and chest, the purpose of this vessel, it is thought, being to receive the freshly extracted hearts of sacrificial victims or other offerings, effectively making the *chacmool* an altar. Behind this *chacmool*, on either side of the path leading to the sanctuary, is a pair of columns fashioned as fearsome-looking Feathered Serpents, whose gaping mouths appear to threaten the viewer from the ground, while the erect tips of their rattlesnakelike tails point toward the sky (the horizontal sections behind these tails, created by kinks in their bodies, would once have supported a lintel over the temple's entrance).

The "Castillo" and the Feathered Serpent

As in many other Maya cities, one of the most imposing edifices at Chichén Itzá is a great pyramid that is variously known as "El Castillo" (Spanish for "The Castle"), the Temple (or Pyramid) of Kukulcan, or the Temple (or Pyramid) of the Feathered Serpent. Having seen it for himself in 1566, Diego de Landa described the "Castillo" as follows: "This structure has four stairways looking to the four directions of the world, and 33 feet wide, with 91 steps to each that are killing to climb. When the stairways thus reach the summit, there is a small flat top, on which was

Above, left: Topped with rectangular capitals, these cylindrical stone columns once held up the roof of the Hall of the Thousand Columns.
Above, right: The square-shaped columns making up the portico in front of the Temple of the Warriors bear depictions of warriors.

a building…" As de Landa observes, the "Castillo," which is set on a square base, has four sides, which were no doubt a symbolic reference to the four quarters of the Maya cosmos. Further aspects of numerical symbolism were incorporated into the "Castillo's" structure, too: when added together, for example, the 91 steps that make up each of the four stairways, plus the "step" represented by the Feathered Serpent heads on the northern side, total 365, the number of days in the solar year. In addition, the nine stages of the "Castillo's" pyramid correspond to the nine levels into which the Maya believed the underworld, *xibalba*, was divided.

In its later form 98 ft (30 m) high (and the edifice that survives to this day was constructed over an earlier pyramid), at the top of the pyramid stands the small temple mentioned by de Landa, whose entrance faces north. Perhaps the most impressive of the "Castillo's" ritual decorative features are the two Feathered Serpent heads that are positioned on either side of the foot of the stairway on the northern side—as noted by de Landa: "When I saw it there was at the foot of the stairways the fierce mouth of a serpent, curiously worked from a single stone"—with their bodies and tails being incorporated into the temple above. The presence of these Feathered Serpents has not only inspired the "Castillo's" alternative names, but has also led scholars to speculate that this sacred construction was dedicated to the god Kukulcan, with whom those within the temple at the pyramid's apex would have hoped to commune. Kukulcan, the Maya divine "Feathered Serpent," corresponded to the Central Mexican Quetzalcoatl, and maybe specifically to Ce Acatl Topiltzin Quetzalcoatl, a historical figure who was revered as the transformer of the city's fortunes following his arrival in Chichén Itzá from Tollán, and also as a patron of the arts, medicine, and the wind, who may have been conflated with the god Quetzalcoatl. One legend relating to Ce Acatl Topiltzin Quetzalcoatl furthermore tells of his ascent into the heavens, where he was transformed into Venus, the "Morning Star."

Two apparently magical aspects of the "Castillo" may reveal themselves to those who know their secret. The first is the play of light and shade cast by the edge of the pyramid at sunset on the equinoxes, which makes it appear as though a sinuous

Right: A chacmool is stationed at the top of the Temple of the Warriors' stairway. Directly behind it is a pair of columns fashioned in the serpentine form of Kukulcan, open jaws resting on the ground and tails pointing heavenward.
Below: A sculpted figure on the wall of the Temple of the Warriors is enclosed by what appear to be feathers incised on the stonework behind it.

Above: Although now partly ruined, the unusual circular shape of the Caracol, or Observatory, remains unmistakable.
Opposite, above: Representations of the Feathered Serpent, known to the Maya as Kukulcan, feature largely at Chichén Itzá, and particularly at the temple dedicated to this deity, the "Castillo."
Opposite, below: The square-sided, temple-topped pyramid that dominates Chichén Itzá's main plaza looks so imposing that the Spanish called it "El Castillo," or "The Castle."

serpentine form comprising seven diamond shapes (like those marking rattlesnakes) is descending the northern side. And the second is the sound, reminiscent of the quetzal bird's call, which is created when a handclap made in front of the Castillo bounces and echoes off the pyramid's steps. These tricks of sound and vision combine references to the divine dual nature of the Feathered Serpent and reinforce the Kukulcan imagery of a rattlesnake with quetzal feathers that is repeatedly seen in the northern, Toltec-influenced part of Chichén Itzá.

The Caracol

Called the Caracol (Spanish for "Snail") on account of the spiral staircase that winds up the partly ruined circular structure to a small chamber at the top, Mayanists believe that this building in the southern, earlier part of Chichén Itzá's ceremonial center functioned as an observatory for the city's astronomers (and maybe also as a temple to Kukulcan). From here, they scrutinized the night sky, tracking the movements of the stars and planets—and particularly of Venus—using little more than a pair of crossed sticks marked with notches as aids to their observations and calculations. Despite their relatively primitive instruments, the Caracol indicates that the astronomers of Chichén Itzá were remarkably knowledgeable, for Mayanists have ascertained that three surviving shafts or windows in the observation chamber are aligned with significant stages in the Venus, solar, and lunar cycles.

The decorative elements that are visible on the round tower's façade—notably those facing each of the four cardinal directions—are typical of the Puuc style of architecture. Yet the building is otherwise quite unusual, comprising as it does concentric circular towers set above two platforms, the highest being almost square, and the lowest, rectangular, suggesting that the Caracol may have been added to over time, and that practicality was more important than esthetic considerations.

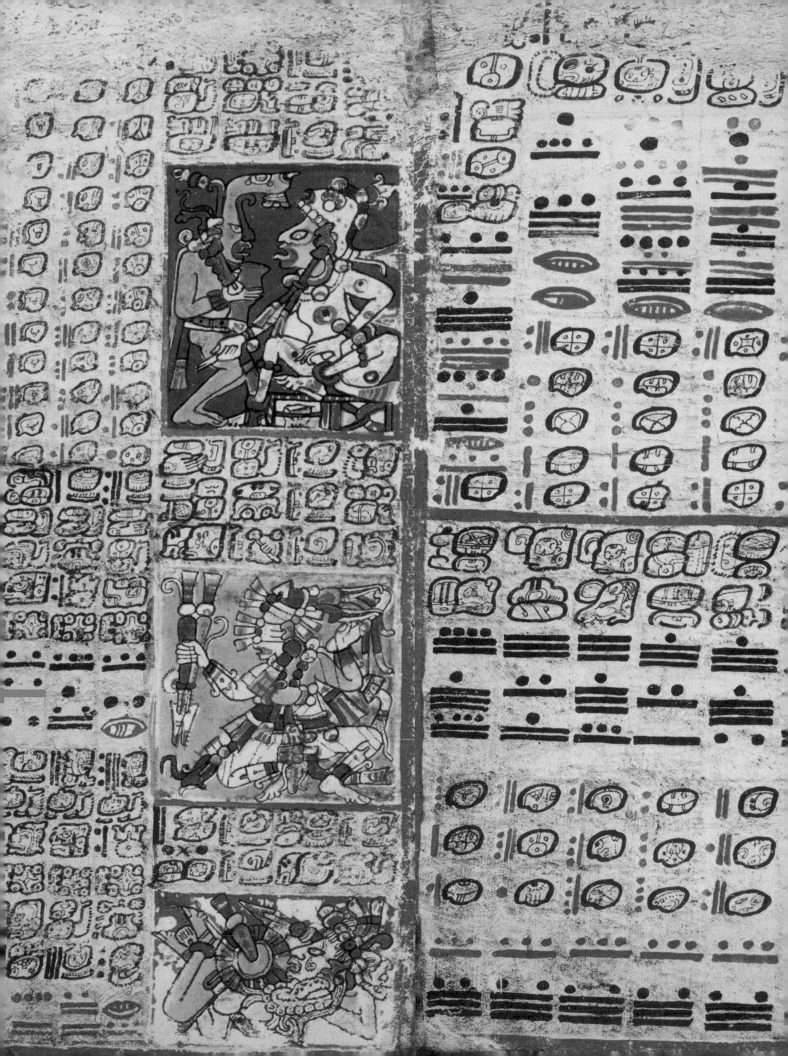

CALENDARS AND COSMOS

The sciences which they taught were the reckoning of the years, months and days, the festivals and ceremonies, the administration of their sacraments, the omens of the days, their methods of divination and prophecies, events, remedies for sickness, antiquities, and the art of reading and writing by their letters and the characters wherewith they wrote, and by pictures that illustrated the writings.

—Diego de Landa, *Relación de las Cosas de Yucatán*, 1566 (*Yucatán Before and After the Conquest*, translation by William Gates).

Opposite: *Page 50 of the Dresden Codex (the Förstemann copy is shown here) is the fifth of the five "Venus pages" that focus on the Venus calendar. The Morning Star (Venus) is represented in the center in figurative form, while the two presiding deities at the top are believed to represent the Maize God and a death god.*

It was not so long ago that many of the meanings of Maya art and writings were a mystery to Mayanists. Because they could not read most of the glyphs that were carved in stone or painted on earthenware or bark paper, they could only hazard informed guesses concerning what any accompanying images portrayed, which was often a hit-or-miss approach. Part of the problem was that they believed the glyphs to be logograms (symbols that represent an entire word or phrase), and only to represent sacred or astronomical concepts. Three crucial breakthroughs came during the 1950s, however, with Yuri Knorosov's proposal that the glyphs also conveyed phonetic information; Heinrich Berlin's identification of Emblem Glyphs; and Tania Proskouriakoff's discovery that the monuments at Piedras Negras recorded historical details relating to the city's rulers. It is largely thanks to the groundbreaking work of these Mayanists—and of those who came after them—that the world of the Maya has been opened up to us. There is still more to be learned, but today we understand far more about how these ancient people viewed the world in which they lived, and how they envisaged their place in it.

Below: *Reproduced below are pages 69, 70, and 71 of the Madrid Codex. The turtle in the top left-hand quarter of page 71 is thought to signify Orion, and to carry the three hearth stones of creation on its back.*

The Maya Cosmos

Symbolized by the unifying World, or Cosmic, Tree (see pages 42 to 46), the Maya believed that the cosmos comprised three major realms: the celestial, the earthly, and the underworld. While humans occupied the earth, the celestial realm was believed to be the home of such sky deities as the Maya Moon Goddess and Kinich Ahau (or God G, the divine embodiment of the sun), as well as of deified ancestors. The underworld (which the Maya called *xibalba*, "place of fright"), by contrast, was thought to be inhabited by the death gods, and to be the first port of call for newly dead Maya. It seems that the heavens were sometimes imagined as having thirteen levels, and the underworld, nine (as represented, for instance, by the nine stages of such pyramids as the "Castillo" constructed at Chichén Itzá: see pages 18 to 31).

The earthly realm was often envisaged as being square, with the World Tree situated at the center, serving as a symbolic *axis mundi* (world axis), and with the central points of each of the four sides oriented toward each of the four cardinal directions: north, south, east, and west. The Quiché Maya sacred book, the *Popol Vuh*, describes "the completion and germination of all the sky and earth—its four corners and its four sides. All then was measured and staked out into four divisions, doubling over and stretching the measuring cords of the womb of sky and the womb of earth. Thus were established the four corners, the four sides ..." The Maya believing themselves to have been created from maize dough, this square earth was likened to a maize field (*milpa*).

Other Maya views of the world conceived of the earth as being either a caiman (see pages 67 to 69) or a turtle, the scutes of whose carapace resemble cracked, dry earth. Indeed, representations of the rebirth of the Maize God from *xibalba* depict him emerging from an earth–turtle (see pages 95 to 97). The Maya furthermore believed that the underworld could be accessed through holes in the earth, with caves, for example, being regarded as entrances to *xibalba*. It also seems that the Maya considered their ballcourts to be portals to the underworld, and that they regarded the Milky Way as a road to *xibalba*.

Opposite: The Paris Codex has suffered some damage over the centuries, as is evident in pages 21, 23, and 24, shown opposite. Mayanists believe that the creatures depicted on pages 23 and 24 represent zodiacal beings.
Below: Copán's ballcourt, which was dedicated in AD 738, is identifiable by its sloping side walls and "I"-shaped playing surface. While the Maya regarded their ballcourts as entrances to the underworld, the ballgame played on them had ritual, mythical, and cosmic significance.

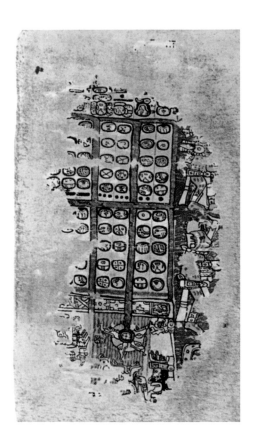 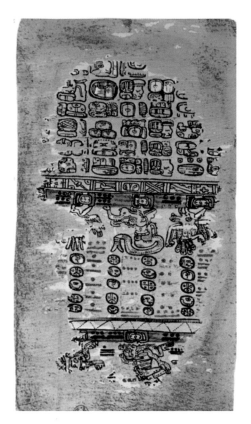 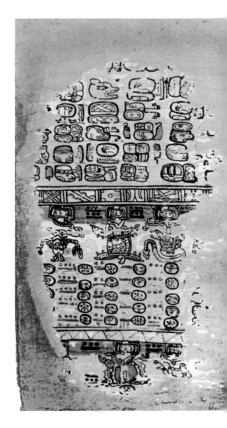

Scrutinizing the Sky

If the ballcourt was believed to provide access to *xibalba*, Mayanists speculate that the ballgame played on it may have had a ritual purpose that referred to the victory of the mythical ballplaying Hero Twins over the *xibalban* death lords, with the ball itself maybe symbolizing the sun. (For more on the Maya ballgame and its possible symbolic significance, see pages 47 to 60.) Their task in *xibalba* done, the *Popol Vuh* tells us that the Hero Twins honored their father, Hun Hunahpu (who corresponds to the Maize God), whose body had been buried at *xibalba*'s Crushing Ballcourt, after which "They arose straight into the sky. One of them rose as the sun, and the other as the moon . . ." It may therefore be that the ritual playing of the ballgame was somehow intended to maintain the positions and course of the sun and the moon.

The Maya certainly focused their attention on the sky, and on the movements of the sun, moon, planets, constellations, and stars. Mayanists believe that at least one surviving building functioned as an observatory—the Caracol at Chichén Itzá in the Yucatán (see pages 22 to 31)—and that Maya observations, and their related astronomical and calendrical calculations and forecasts, were impressively accurate, despite their lack of technically advanced equipment.

Certain celestial objects were considered to be more significant than others, also being interpreted rather differently to how we do today. The constellations of the Maya zodiac differed from those of the Western zodiac, for one thing (a turtle, for example, representing the constellation of Orion, see pages 164 to 167), while eclipses were greatly feared, being seen as "bitings," with no certainty that the sun or moon being eclipsed would survive unscathed. Although the Maya regarded it as a star, the planet Venus seems to have given them most cause for concern on account of the destructive influence that it was thought to bear on the earth below (see pages 64 to 66). During its 584-day synodic cycle—that is, it includes two successive conjunctions—Venus was believed to descend into *xibalba* (during its superior conjunction), followed by its appearance as the Evening Star, and then by a time of invisibility (its inferior conjunction), after which it entered its Morning Star phase, the time when it was believed to present the greatest danger.

horoscopes, as described by Diego de Landa in his sixteenth-century narrative, *Relación de las Cosas de Yucatán (An Account of the Things of Yucatán/Yucatán Before and After the Conquest)*: "When the children were born, they bathed them at once, and then when the pain of pressing the foreheads and heads was over, they took them to the priest that he might cast their fate, declare the office the child was to fill, and give him the name he was to retain during his childhood …" It seems that it was primarily the day on which he or she was born, according to the *tzolkin*, or 260-day calendar, that was thought to determine a Maya child's character and destiny in life. (Often described as a ritual calendar, or almanac, the 260-day calendar was used by other Mesoamerican peoples, too, including the Aztec—see pages 198 to 201—who, however, called it, and its day signs, different names.) The fundamental components of the *tzolkin* were twenty day signs, or day names (see pages 40 to 41), and thirteen day numbers (1 to 13), which, when used in conjunction—as 1 Imix, 2 Ik', 3 Akbal, and so on—produced a 260-day cycle during which no combination of day name and number was the same.

Another calendar used by the Maya was the *haab*, or 365-day "vague-year" calendar, which was more useful for day-to-day activities because the *tzolkin* did not correspond to the solar year. The *haab* consisted of eighteen twenty-day months, plus an inauspicious five-day period (*uayeb*) that preceded the start of the new year (see pages 76 to 77). (The glyphs representing these months and the *uayeb* are shown on pages 40 to 41.) When operating in combination, the *tzolkin* and the *haab* produced the Calendar Round, a 52-year cycle during which no date repeated itself, which was invaluable for keeping track of the passing of the (solar) years.

There was, however, another calendar designed to track even longer periods of time, as wonderingly, if confusingly, described by de Landa:

Tracking Time

Their dread of the catastrophes that might be unleashed by a solar or lunar eclipse, or by Venus, was a vital reason why the Maya developed an array of calendars with which to try to track and predict inauspicious times. These included a lunar calendar (which Mayanists call the Lunar Series) and the "Lords of the Night" cycle, known as the "G" series and comprising the nine deities who were believed to govern the night-time hours. Forewarned is forearmed, in the view of the Maya, and foreknowledge of Venus's likely movements, for instance, would at least allow them to limit or harness its damaging powers, they thought. More positively, they believed that auspicious days and periods could be similarly foretold, and that the appropriate rituals could then be performed, or festivals celebrated, to take advantage of the ideal cosmic conditions for sowing maize, for example.

Such prophecies were the particular province of Maya priests (see pages 184 to 185), who were also responsible for casting newborn children's

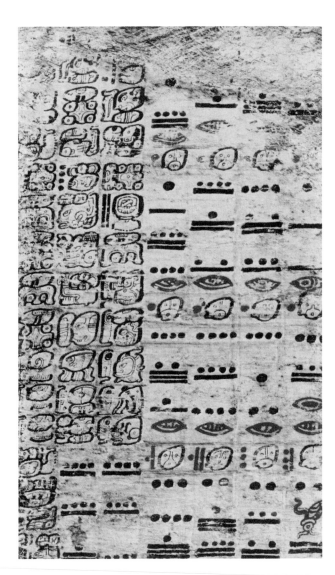

Opposite: This fanciful modern artifact combines the two outer circles of the Aztec Sun Stone (see pages 198 to 201) with an inner ring containing glyphs representing the eighteen twenty-day months of the Maya haab *(365-day calendar), plus the five-day* uayeb *period. A profile portrait of the Maize God can be seen at the center.*

Left and below: A series of glyphs and numbers appear on pages 24 (left) and 51 (below) of the Madrid codex.

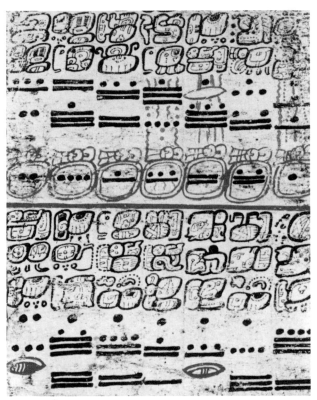

Not only did the Indians have a count for the year and months, as has been before set out, but they also had a certain method of counting time and their matters by ages, which they counted by 20-year periods, counting thirteen twenties, with one of the twenty signs in their months, which they call Ahau, not in order, but going backwards as appears in the following circular design. In their language they call these periods katuns, with these making a calculation of ages that it is marvelous; thus it was easy for the old man of whom I spoke in the first chapter to recall events which he said had taken place 300 years before. Had I not known of this calculation I should not have believed it possible to recall after such a period.

Known as the Long Count by Mayanists, the 5125-year-long calendar cycle mentioned by de Landa was charted by means of five periods, respectively called *kin* (which equaled 1 day); *uinal* (which corresponded to 20 *kins*, or 20 days); *tun* (which comprised 18 *uinals*, making 360 days); *katun* (the equivalent of 20 *tuns*, and therefore 7200 days); and *baktun* (the name for 20 *katuns*, or 144,000 days); see page 41 for the glyphs that represent these five periods. The Maya celebrated Long Count period-ending dates (see, for instance, pages 146 to 148), and it is reckoned that the starting date of the current Long Count cycle was in August 3114 BC, and that it is due to end in December 2012. According to convention, Mayanists record this end date in Arabic numerals, starting with the highest period, as falling on 13.0.0.0.0 (that is, 13 *baktuns*, plus 0 *katuns*, plus 0 *tuns*, plus 0 *uinals*, plus 0 *kins*).

A Matter of Record

In order to record significant calendrical dates, be it for purposes of prognostication or as a matter of historical record, the Maya developed a sophisticated writing system comprising hieroglyphs, or glyphs (which Mayanists now believe to be logosyllabic, or a combination of logograms and syllabograms, which represent syllables), a variety of which you'll spot within the works presented in this book.

Although glyphs representing gods' heads, and sometimes also their bodies, were used to represent numbers (certain deities being considered patrons of specific numbers) on grand and elaborate monuments, a far simpler, dot-and-bar notation system was more generally used (see page 41 for an indication of how this system worked, as well as for an indication of how 0 was represented).

Such glyphs and numerical notations are frequently seen on the stelae erected within the ceremonial complexes of Maya cities to commemorate significant dates and occasions of dynastic importance, being described by de Landa as the focal point for sacrificial rituals: "To make these sacrifices in the courts of the temples there were erected certain tall decorated posts …" (see, for example, pages 78 to 79). They were also inscribed on other important stone monuments, such as lintels, altars, and wall panels, as part of murals (as, for example, at the significant Late Preclassic site at San Bartolo, Guatemala), and on the ceramic vessels that often accompanied the Maya to the grave. And according to de Landa, they were written in books, too:

These people also used certain characters or letters, with which they wrote in their books about the antiquities and their sciences; with these, and with figures, and certain signs in the figures, they understood their matters, made them known, and taught them. We found a great number of books in these letters, and since they contained nothing but superstitions and falsehoods of the devil, we burned them all, which they took most grievously and which gave them great pain.

The burning of the Maya books by the Spanish was a tragic loss—to the Maya, and to the Mayanists who would have learned so much from them. Only four escaped the conflagration to exemplify de Landa's description of the books that are today called codices: "They wrote their books on a long sheet doubled in folds, which was then enclosed between two boards finely ornamented; the writing was on one side and the other, according to

the folds. The paper they made from the roots of the tree, and gave it a white finish excellent for writing upon." The paper having been thus carefully prepared, trained scribes then used brushes and pigments with which to write and illustrate their subjects.

Apart from that of the Grolier, which is named after New York City's Grolier Club, where it was exhibited following its discovery, the names of the surviving Maya codices, which date from the Postclassic Period, relate to the cities where they are now housed (the Grolier Codex today being in Mexico City). Although their general themes revolve around astronomical observances, calendars, and the performance of rituals, the four surviving codices vary somewhat in their subject matter. The Grolier Codex, which came to light during the 1960s, appears to be mainly a Venus almanac, for instance, while the Paris Codex additionally contains information relating to *katuns*, as well as to new-year rituals and to the zodiac. The Dresden Codex, which was discovered in Madrid,

Spain, in 1739, but is now located in Dresden, Germany, includes a notable Venus calendar and eclipse tables (for some examples of pages from the Dresden Codex, see pages 61 to 69). And the Madrid Codex (which is sometimes called the Tro–Cortesianus Codex, having once been separated into sections called the Troano and the Cortesianus) is also notable for its detailed almanacs and for the information on new-year and other rituals that it presents (some pages from the Madrid Codex can be seen on pages 70 to 77 and pages 102 to 105).

Not only are they rare and important documents, but the four surviving Maya codices are also dismayingly fragile, as was sadly demonstrated during World War II, when the Dresden Codex suffered significant water damage during the bombing of the city. It is therefore fortunate that detailed facsimiles are available to Mayanists to study, made by such dedicated individuals as Lord Edward Kingsborough (who commissioned a noted copy of the Dresden Codex, as did Ernst Förstemann), Léon de Rosny (who was responsible for copying the Paris Codex and the Cortesianus section of the Madrid Codex) and the Abbé C. E. Brasseur de Bourbourg (who reproduced the Troano part of the Madrid Codex), and, more recently, Justin Kerr (who photographed the Grolier Codex; a few examples of his "rollout" photographs of ceramic vessels appear in this book).

SOME CALENDRICAL AND NUMERICAL MAYA GLYPHS

The glyphs that the Maya used to symbolize days, months, and longer periods of time, as well as numbers, can be seen carved into stone monuments like stelae, painted on cylinder vessels, and inscribed within the surviving codices.

The Twenty Day Names of the *Tzolkin*

Shown below are the glyphs representing the twenty day names, or day signs, of the Maya 260-day calendar (the *tzolkin*), which operated in conjunction with thirteen numbers.

imix *ik'* *akbal* *kan*

chicchan *cimi* *manik* *lamat*

muluc *oc* *chuen* *eb*

ben *ix* *men* *cib*

caban *edznab* *cauac* *ahau*

The Nineteen Months of the Haab

The glyphs that represented the nineteen months of the *haab*, the 360-day calendar of the Maya, are shown below. The first eighteen months each consisted of twenty days, with the last, *uayeb*, comprising five days.

pop *uo* *zip* *zotz'*

zec *xul* *yaxkin* *mol*

ch'en *yax* *zac* *ceh*

mac *kankin* *muan* *pax*

kayab *cumku* *uayeb*

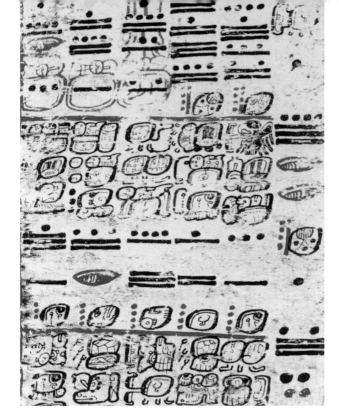

Above, opposite and below, right: Pages from the Dresden Codex showing a selection of numerical and calendrical glyphs. Such notations are also seen on many of the stelae that have been discovered at ancient Maya sites.

The Five Periods of the Long Count

Five glyphs, illustrated below, represented the periods that made up the Long Count structure.

kin (1 day)

uinal (20 x *kins* = 20 days)

tun (18 x *uinals* = 360 days)

katun (20 x *tuns* = 7200 days)

baktun (20 x *katuns* = 144,000 days)

The Maya Numbering System

Shown below are the elements of the dot-and-bar notation, the simplest of the Maya methods for recording numbers. Numbers could also be represented by the more elaborate head variants (showing the heads of deities) and by full-figure glyphs (showing the heads and bodies of deities), with an alternative for 0 being half of a glyph resembling a four-petaled flower, or quatrefoil.

0	⬭	10	══
1	•	11	══
2	••	12	══
3	•••	13	═══
4	••••	14	═══
5	──	15	═══
6	•──	16	═══
7	••──	17	═══
8	•••──	18	═══
9	••••──	19	═══

The Lid of King Pacal's Sarcophagus

c.AD 683

Carved limestone, Temple of Inscriptions, Palenque, Chiapas, Mexico

One of the most spectacular finds ever made by archeologists investigating a Maya site was the funerary crypt of King Pacal at Palenque. The burial chamber was discovered at the bottom of a concealed stairway deep within the nine-level pyramid on which the Temple of Inscriptions was constructed on Pacal's orders some time during his long reign, which began in AD 615 and ended with his death in 683. Numerous treasures had been interred alongside Pacal (see, for example, pages 154 to 155), but none was quite as spectacular—or as valuable an aid to scholars—as the rectangular limestone lid measuring around 12 x 7 feet that covered the sarcophagus containing the dead king's body. For as the photograph opposite shows (and is more clearly illustrated by the drawing on page 44), it was completely covered in incised bas-relief glyphs and images that, it transpired, illustrated the Maya perception of the cosmos.

The bands running down the sides of the stone slab represent the sky, with the *kin* glyph in the northeastern corner signifying the sun (which rises in the east) and day, and the *akbal* glyph in the northwestern corner denoting darkness and night, the west being where the setting sun seems to sink into the underworld every evening. Indeed, the course of Pacal's entire life, from birth to death, can be compared to the sun's passage across the sky, with the red-colored cinnabar that was brushed over the lid also suggesting life and renewal: red is both the hue of blood and the color that the Maya linked with the east, where the sun is "reborn" each day. Beneath a strip of glyphs and portraits that may depict previous rulers of Palenque can be seen the Principal Bird Deity. This celestial bird perches on the World Tree, or Cosmic Tree, whose trunk unites the heavens, the earthly world, and the underworld, which the Maya called *xibalba* ("place of fright"). Pacal is pictured at the moment of his death, in freefall as he slides down the World Tree's trunk, which one theory has equated with the Milky Way in this scene. While it appears that Pacal has just entered the underworld, it may alternatively be that he is on the verge of bursting out of *xibalba* and that he is about to be reborn into divine immortality. Certainly, Pacal expected to follow in the footsteps of the Maize God, who, as Hun Hunahpu, died at the hands of the death gods in *xibalba*, according to Maya belief, later being resurrected by his sons, the Hero Twins, and being reborn through a crack in the earth (see pages 95 to 97).

See also **Relief Showing a Seated Man Wearing Magnificent Robes and a Headdress of Feathers** (pages 154 to 155).

Mayanists have identified the glyph (above) in the northwestern corner, opposite the *kin* glyph, as *akbal,* meaning "darkness." The glyphs that have been inscribed in the vertical sky band below this are associated with the night.

The human heads that have been carved in profile along the upper and lower borders of the sarcophagus lid are thought to represent Pacal's predecessors as Palenque's rulers.

The *kin* glyph inscribed in the northeastern corner denotes the sun, or the day. Another *kin* glyph can be seen at the center of the vertical sky band below it.

The top glyph of the lid's left-hand sky band (right) represents the planet Venus (*ek'*; see also pages 64 to 66.)

This glyph (right) signifies the moon.

If the World Tree represents the Milky Way within this image, and the double-headed serpent, the ecliptic, the point at which they cross may have cosmic symbolism, representing, perhaps, the point of creation.

The enormous bird (above) that is perched on top of the World Tree has been identified by Mayanists as the Principal Bird Deity, a divine celestial bird thought to be an early form of the ancient creator god Itzamna. The Principal Bird Deity may also correspond to Vucub Caquix, or 7 Macaw, who once proclaimed himself the sun and moon, according to the Quiché Maya creation account, the *Popol Vuh*. (See also pages 50 to 55 and 92 to 94.)

Believed to be a ceiba tree (or silk-cotton tree), but sometimes depicted as a maize plant, the World Tree's trunk is decorated with glyphic elements thought to denote mirrors. These are also seen on Maya portrayals of gods, usually on their limbs, such "god-markings" suggesting supernatural beings.

The body of a heavily decorated double-headed serpent curves across the World Tree's trunk. Its two heads (details above) are positioned on either side of the tree, jaws agape, with gods emerging from their mouths: K'awil can be seen on the left, and the Jester God, on the right. This creature has been symbolically linked by scholars with the ecliptic, the Milky Way, and the sky, as well as with the ceremonial bar that Maya kings are frequently portrayed holding, and thus with rulership. (See also pages 78 to 79 and 95 to 97.)

King Pacal is portrayed in the process of falling, with his back facing downward. Unless it was as captives, Maya kings were never usually portrayed in such an apparently humiliating, helplessly unbalanced position. This has been interpreted in two ways: firstly, as the instant of Pacal's death, in which case he is plummeting toward the underworld; and, secondly, as the moment of his resurrection, in which case he is re-emerging from the underworld and is heading rapidly for the heavens.

The World Tree stands strong and tall as it points toward the north. Called *wakah-chan* ("raised-up sky"), the World Tree was envisaged as having been used to separate the sky from the earth at the time of creation. A pair of horizontal branches and the trunk create a cross shape, which may refer to the Maya belief that the cosmos was square in shape, and divided into four quarters. At the end of each branch can be seen a square-nosed serpent, along with series of dots that may symbolize drops of blood; the earthly realm may be indicated here.

This section of the tree trunk is reminiscent of the glyph that means "tree": *te'*.

The profile view of Pacal's face demonstrates that it conforms to the Maya ideal of perfection based on the supposed appearance of the Maize God, that is, with a smoothly curving line running upward and backward from the tip of his nose to the crown of his head. (And on examining Pacal's corpse, archeologists found that his skull had been deliberately deformed to create this shape.) Like the Maize God, Pakal is pictured in the prime of life, even though he was an old man when he died.

The object that projects from just above Pacal's forehead is a ceremonial mirror or ax, while the element that curves away from it to the right represents smoke. When seen affixed to the forehead, this smoking mirror or ax is usually an attribute of K'awil (who equates to God K, God II of the Palenque Triad, and the Manikin Scepter, see also pages 98 to 99, 106 to 108, and 146 to 148). K'awil was regarded as a divine patron of royal dynasties, and this connection indicates that Pacal in turn was considered a divine monarch. In addition, K'awil's links with fire and lightning, as represented by this smoking ax, suggest transformation, and particularly the transition that Pacal is undergoing here, between the world of the living and that of the dead.

The beaded net skirt that Pacal is wearing connects him with the Maize God, who may be depicted dressed in it in scenes in which he is shown dancing out of *xibalba*. This type of skirt was usually worn by Maya women, but adorns the Maize God to signify his powers of fertility. Pacal would have expected to have emulated the Maize God in being resurrected following his death.

Indeed, when this sarcophagus lid was removed, the dead king was found to be dressed like the Maize God, and to be covered in a mask and jewelry made of jade, a substance associated in the Maya mind with both maize and eternal life.

The sides that curve around Pacal and the teeth, flanked by a pair of fangs, at the bottom (see detail below), indicate that the dead king has either just entered, or is on the point of emerging from, the skeletal jaws of a monstrous being whose body leads to the underworld. Some Mayanists call this monster, whose maw is an entrance to *xibalba*, the White-Bone-Snake. Its overall shape resembles a glyph (tentatively identified as *japay*) that signifies the portal to the underworld.

Mayanists have identified the object on which Pacal seems to be balancing as a "deified" sacrificial vessel, in other words, a bowl (or plate) containing items associated with sacrificial offerings. Here, they are a *Spondylus* (spiny-oyster) shell, a stingray spine or shark's tooth, and the *cimi* glyph, the sixth of the day signs of the 260-day calendar, or *tzolkin*, which means "death." This sacrificial bowl and its contents seem to be worn as a headdress by a divine being, with huge, spiral-containing "god-eyes." Mayanists call this deity the Quadripartite God and think it may be the sun god's partially skeletal, or God C, aspect.

Maya Ballcourt Marker 591 AD

Limestone, from Chinkultic, Chiapas, Museo National de Antropologia, Mexico City, Mexico

The significance of the limestone ballcourt marker that was discovered at La Esperanza, Chinkultic, in Chiapas, extends far beyond providing evidence that the Maya incorporated such roundels into their ballcourts for the purposes of scoring or demarcation. Although this is indeed an important consideration, the marker's real value to Mayanists lies in two considerations: firstly, in the clear visual link that it makes between the events described in the *Popol Vuh* (the Quiché Maya creation account) and the ritual nature of the Maya ballgame (see also pages 50 to 60); and, secondly, in the information provided by the glyphs encircling its circumference and those displayed within its inner circle.

It is the marker's imagery that first catches the eye, and particularly the large circle abutting the strangely contorted lower half of the central figure's body. In fact, the man's position and protective clothing tell us that he is engaged in the Maya ballgame, and that the circle represents the rubber ball that was used in the game. The disembodied head that has been incised within the ball is a reference to the episode in the *Popol Vuh* in which the Hero Twin Xbalanque is forced to take part in a ballgame against the death gods of the underworld—*xibalba* ("place of fright")—when the decapitated head of his brother, Hunahpu, is initially used as a ball. The connection is not quite understood, but it seems that the head-as-ball image may also symbolically refer to the movements of the sun and moon (which the Hero Twins eventually rose into the heavens to become), and especially with that of the sun, while the marker itself may represent an opening to *xibalba*. It may therefore be that the ultimate purpose of the Maya ballgame was to ensure that the powers of light and life continued to prevail over those of darkness and death.

Although it evokes a sacred story, and sacred symbolism, the ballcourt marker is also a commemorative monument, for the glyphs encircling the edge set out a Long Count date of 9.7.17.12.14 and a Calendar Round (52-year cycle) date of 11 *ix* 7 *zotz'*. Corresponding as this does to May 17, 591 AD, the inscription suggests that the ballcourt was dedicated on this day. In addition, the two vertically positioned sets of glyphs suggest that the ballplayer is most likely to be Chinkultic's ruler.

See also **Cylindrical Vases Depicting Ballplayers and a Ballgame** (pages 50 to 60).

This (above) is the *zotz'* glyph, which symbolizes the fourth month of the Maya *haab* (the 365-day "vague-year" calendar).

Elements of the ballplayer's headdress have been symbolically linked with the lords of *xibalba*, including a water lily (*Nymphaea*) and a jaguar's tail, both of which may symbolise the watery, dark, and dangerous underworld realm.

The head that is portrayed within the large ball is believed to be that of Hunahpu, the Hero Twin whose head was used as a ball by the death gods of *xibalba*. It is thought that the Maya may have used the skulls of decapitated captives to serve as the centers of the rubber balls that they used for the ballgame, which may in turn have been a ritual re-enactment of the Hero Twins' mythical ballgame. (See also ball detail, page 60.)

The ballgame player is dressed in a wide protective belt. The belts that were worn by those participating in the ballgame were probably made from wood, leather, and padding; those belts whose sole function was as ceremonial garb—called "yokes," on account of their "U" shapes—were, by contrast, made from stone (see yoke detail, page 59).

This is the Introductory Glyph that introduces the Long Count date, which is written in a pattern called the Initial Series.

The ballgame player has braced his body for impact with the large, heavy ball. According to ballgame rules, contact with the ball could only be made with the head and torso, hips, thighs, and knees, and with the upper arms and shoulders, but not with the hands or feet.

Cylindrical Vessel Depicting Ballplayers and the Journey to *Xibalba*

c. 600–900 AD

Earthenware, Chrysler Museum of Art, Norfolk, Virginia

Painted as it actually is around the outer surface of a cylindrical polychrome vessel, sections of the complex image shown here inevitably remain invisible to viewers contemplating the artifact itself. And while the panoramic format of this "rollout" photograph (a two-dimensional rendering of the vase) allows one to take them in at a glance, the four scenes that encircle the vase remain somehow distinct from one another. All are nevertheless linked through the allusions that they make to the Maya underworld—called *xibalba* ("place of fright")—as well as to episodes from the *Popol Vuh*, the creation account of the Quiché Maya.

The black balls that they hold identify the two central figures as ballplayers, in all likelihood either the Hero Twins (Hunahpu and Xbalanque) or their father (Hun Hunahpu, or 1 Hunahpu) and his brother (Vucub Hunahpu, or 7 Hunahpu), all of whom were keen ballplayers, according to the *Popol Vuh*. An alternative reading is that the lighter-skinned figure on the right is one of these characters, but that his adversary is one of the death gods who challenged (on separate occasions) the two sets of brothers to descend to *xibalba* to take part in a ballgame.

Another significant section can be seen on the far right, where a monstrous human–tree hybrid supports a large bird between its crossed branches. The *Popol Vuh* tells of just such a bird, Vucub Caquix, or 7 Macaw (which Mayanists equate with the Principal Bird Deity), who falsely claimed to be the sun and moon, but was shot to the ground by the Hero Twins as he ate fruit in a nance tree, after which the replacement of his damaged teeth with maize and the plucking-out of his eyes led to his eventual death.

In referring to the ballgame (which may itself symbolize the movement of the sun and moon), and, more specifically, to the Hero Twins' destruction of Vucub Caquix, the scenes painted on this vase emphasize the ultimate victory of the forces of life over those of death. This would therefore have been a symbolically apt vessel to accompany a recently deceased Maya individual to the grave—and beyond, initially to *xibalba*, and then, if the horrors of the underworld were survived, to regeneration in the heavens, following the path of the Hero Twins, who rose to the sky to become the true sun and moon.

See also **Maya Ballcourt Marker** (pages 47 to 49).

The glyphs running along the top of the vessel's outer rim form the Primary Standard Sequence (PSS), a formulaic series of glyphs that is typically seen on Maya ceramics. They provide information about how the vessel was made, by whom, for what purpose, and for whom.

His Roman nose, toothless mouth, and aged appearance identify the older male at right as Itzamna (who is equated with God D in the Schellhas system of nomenclature; see also pages 92 to 94). The Maya considered Itzamna to be a creator god, and thus the oldest and most senior of their deities.

Although it is not certain exactly who the black-hued ballplayer shown below is, his sombrero hat—to the Maya, the sign of a hunter—suggests that he is one of the Hero Twins. They were adept users of the clay-pellet-firing blowgun (see pages 113 to 115).

It is clear from the abject gesture that he makes as he gazes up at the god above him, and also from his subjugation literally underfoot, that the man shown above is the captive of the black figure who towers over him. The black patches on his body, and his headband, may mark him out as Hunahpu.

The monstrous, headlike throne on which Itzamna sits includes jaguar-skin elements like this shown below. The Maya associated the jaguar with both royalty and the underworld.

As they stand facing each other, the central figures each grasp a black ball in one hand. Black rubber balls like these were used in the Maya ballgame (see also page 60).

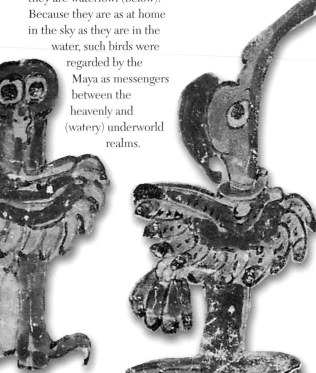

The extraordinarily long bills of two of the diametrically opposed birds suggest that they are waterfowl (below). Because they are as at home in the sky as they are in the water, such birds were regarded by the Maya as messengers between the heavenly and (watery) underworld realms.

Two of the four birds that occupy a section of the vase appear to be round-eyed owls, birds of the night. The *Popol Vuh* relates that the lords of *xibalba* sent messenger owls to summon 1 Hunahpu and 7 Hunahpu and, later, the Hero Twins, to the underworld.

The bird that can be seen between the branches of a supernatural tree (above)—which may symbolize the world or cosmic tree, see pages 44 to 46—is Vucub Caquix (7 Macaw), or the Principal Bird Deity, whose long-drawn-out demise was initiated by his shooting with clay pellets by the Hero Twins. Despite his name, Vucub Caquix is never depicted as a macaw, but resembles a king vulture.

This glyph is the Initial Sign, which signals the start of the Primary Standard Sequence (PSS) text. (See another Initial Sign on page 59.)

Cylindrical Vessel Depicting a Ballgame c. 600–900 AD

Earthenware, Chrysler Museum of Art, Norfolk, Virginia

It may have featured a ball and opposing teams, but the Maya ballgame, as depicted on this polychrome ceramic vessel, had a far more serious function than merely providing sporting entertainment—indeed, it was believed to have cosmic significance. The ballgame's importance is based on the events related in the *Popol Vuh*, the Quiché Maya creation story, where it is told how the Hero Twins, Hunahpu and Xbalanque, and before them their father, Hun Hunahpu, and his twin brother, Vucub Hunahpu, were summoned by the death gods to play the ballgame against them in the underworld (*xibalba*, or "place of fright"). After many setbacks, the Hero Twins eventually vanquished the death gods and ascended from *xibalba* to the heavens, where they became the sun and moon (see also pages 47 to 55).

It seems that the Maya ballgame assumed ritual significance partly because the ballplaying Hero Twins were believed to have become the heavenly bodies associated with day and night, and partly because Hun Hunahpu was equated with the Maya Maize God (see pages 95 to 97). It was therefore considered imperative that these forces of light and life should continue to prevail over the pestilence- and death-bringing lords of *xibalba*. This was encouraged by ritual re-enactments of the ballgame described in the *Popol Vuh*. Indeed, the ball may have represented the sun itself, while the ballcourt may have symbolized the entrance to *xibalba*, and a ballgame victory may have denoted the resurrection of the Maize God and thus the assured germination and growth of the future maize crop.

Maya cities had at least one ballcourt, which was often constructed on a north–south axis in the shape of an "I," the longer section being enclosed by parallel sloping or vertical walls made of earth or stone. Markers could be set into the ground (these may have been regarded as portals to *xibalba*), with one or more circular rings being positioned high on a wall flanking the long, straight field of play. The two teams probably each comprised two or more players, who struck the ball with their bodies—ideally with the hips—but not with their hands or feet, their aim being to score "goals," perhaps by hitting a marker or else by sending the ball through a sidewall ring or into an end zone. It appears that some players were captives, and also that a ballgame's losers could be sacrificed as an offering to the gods, their decapitated heads sometimes being incorporated into new balls or else being displayed, like trophies, on skull racks.

See also **Maya Ballcourt Marker** (pages 47 to 49).

Although it resembles the long-handled feathered fans used by the Maya, this large, circular object is more likely to be a battle standard that has been symbolically placed on the ballcourt to signal the nature of the conflict taking place here. The ballgame may have been regarded as ritual warfare—and it may be that actual battles were re-enacted through the playing of the ballgame.

The band of glyphs that has been painted around the outer rim of this ceramic vessel is known as the Primary Standard Sequence (PSS), this being an inscription that provides information about the vessel itself rather than scene depicted below.

As its name suggests, this glyph, the Initial Sign, marks the start of the sequence (see a similar one on page 55).

Both ballplayers wear cumbersome belts designed to protect their vital organs from the potentially catastrophic damage that may be inflicted by a heavy rubber ball traveling at speed.

Such body protectors were made from wood, leather, and padding, unless they were intended for ceremonial purposes only, in which case these "yokes" (so called on account of their shape, which left them open at one side) were created from stone.

He may be dressed similarly to his opponent, but the lack of feathers surmounting his headdress and his less elaborate clothing together suggest that the ballplayer on the left is of a lower social status.

This figure wears a headdress that appears to have been modeled on the head of a deer, an animal that the Maya hunted and whose flesh they also offered to the gods. The umbrellalike element of the headdress that emerges from the deer's mouth has been identified as a water lily (*Nymphaea*), a plant that the Maya associated with such concepts as water, creation, and a living link between the earthly world and the watery underworld.

The vertical columns of glyphs that have been inserted within the spaces that punctuate the vessel's figurative elements are called secondary texts. Secondary texts typically provide narrative information concerning the characters and events portrayed on ceramic vessels.

The stepped structure behind the ballplayers (below) represents one side of the ballcourt. Such terraces may have provided seating for spectators, or a tiered platform for sacrifices, with sacrificial victims being bound into ball-like shapes and hurled from the top to the bottom.

A large, black rubber ball serves as the scene's focal point. Made from the sap of the rubber tree (*Castilla elastica*), the balls used in Maya ballgames varied in size, but were thought to have measured anything from 6 to 18 in. (around 15 to 46 cm) in diameter, and to have weighed, on average, 8 lb (3.6 kg). It is possible that some balls were built up around centers formed by human skulls (see also page 48).

Protective shin pads have been tied to the players' knees (below). Shin pads and knee pads—often fashioned from padded deerskin—were standard wear for Maya ballplayers, who might also wear padded gloves, forearm or elbow protectors, hip pads, and helmets.

Maya kings robed themselves in jaguar-skin tunics on going into battle, so the pelt suggests that this ballplayer is a royal combatant. The jaguar represented kingship and strength, as well as the underworld, to the Maya, and it is known that Maya kings participated either actually or ritually in the ballgame. (See also page 76.)

This extravagant headdress is based on the head of a waterfowl that appears to have snatched a fish from the water and is still grasping it in its long, sharp bill. Not only does this image convey the idea of a successful predator, but water birds were associated with both the heavens and the underworld in Maya minds.

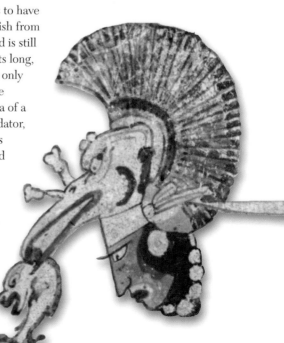

Page 6 from the Dresden Codex

Thirteenth, fourteenth, or fifteenth century

Painted bark paper, Sächsische Landesbibliothek, Dresden, Germany

Shown here and on the following pages is page 6 of the Dresden Codex, with its complex combination of dots and bars, glyphs, and deity figures. The section of the codex that includes this page is filled with numerous almanacs that predict good and bad days on which to perform certain activities. These prognostications, which characteristically extend over 260 days (that is, over the calendrical cycle known as the *tzolkin*), appear to be influenced by the particular deities that preside over particular sets of days. A pattern of alternating positive and negative influences can be discerned by Mayanists within this page and others, so that, for example, while the outcome represented by Itzamna, the left-hand figure in the central row of divine personifications seen here, is stated as being positive, that signified by God Q, directly to Itzamna's right, is negative, while the prediction associated with the Maize God, on the far right, is again positive.

The dots and bars that have been positioned between the horizontal rows of glyphs and the rectangles containing portraits of the divine beings denote numbers—a dot means "1," while a bar equals "5"—and thus certain days within the cycle, according to the combination used. The glyphs that appear in a vertical column to the left of the deities seated on the far right within the bottom two horizontal rows of figures represent some of the *tzolkin*'s twenty day names, while the glyphs presented in horizontal lines are concerned with conveying the prognostications themselves. As neatly set out as the page's various components are (and the Dresden Codex is especially admired by Mayanists for the quality of its calligraphy and artistry), it would still have required significant skill and experience on the part of priestly interpreters to make the correct calendrical calculations and to interpret the almanacs' meanings and messages accurately. And such was the perceived immutability of each day's influences that if an error was made in deciding that a certain day would be auspicious for fishing, for instance, it seems that a fisherman would inevitably have been doomed to failure if he set out on a quest to secure a catch on that day.

See also **Page 51 from the Madrid Codex** (pages 70 to 71).

Four dots mean "4," according to the Maya system of recording numbers.

In the depiction of God R above (top left of the codex page), his identifying mark of a *caban* "curl"—the element that can also be seen within the *caban*, "earth," day sign, the *tzolkin*'s seventeenth—is visible on his cheek. God R's associations are with earth and the number 11.

The central seated figure in the top tier of Maya deities has been identified as God H, a young male god about whom Mayanists know little, but believe may have been connected with the wind. He is shown here wearing a necklace of large beads, along with other forms of jewelry, and holding aloft what is thought to be a plant.

The black line extending from his visible eye and the curving division mark on his cheek (which differentiate him from God A, bottom right on the codex page) suggest that this is the death deity God A' (below).

Recognizable by his roman nose, "god-eye," and aged appearance, the deity shown below is Itzamna (God D in the Schellhas system of naming), an old creator god to whom the Maya accorded great importance. They regarded him as a priestly deity and the inventor of writing. Another distinctive feature with which Itzamna is often portrayed, and which may have been included in this representation, is a disk on his forehead that incorporates the *akbal* ("darkness") glyph, signifying the third day sign in the *tzolkin*. This may represent an obsidian mirror, reflecting the mastery of scrying and divination with which Itzamna was credited (see also pages 92 to 94).

The curving band that marks the face above indicates that this is God Q, a deity who in Maya minds was linked with aggression, death, and destruction, as well as with the number 10. Seen drilling a fire stick between his hands in order to a create a flame (see also pages 70 to 71), the object into which he is drilling the rod is actually the *manik* ("deer") glyph, which resembles a grasping hand and symbolizes the seventh of the *tzolkin*'s day signs.

This (right) is the *lamat* ("Venus") glyph, which represents the eighth of the *tzolkin*'s day signs.

The deity with the rather simian head who is shown striding forward in the bottom left-hand corner of the codex page is God C (right), the deity who embodied the concepts of "god" and "sacredness" (*kuh* and *kuhul*) to the Maya.

His fine, well-muscled body, splendid headdress, necklace, and other personal adornments, along with his serene expression and elongated head, identify the divine person below as the Maize God (or God E), otherwise known as the resurrected Hun Hunahpu, father of the Hero Twins, of which the *Popol Vuh* (the Quiché Maya creation story) tells. The Maize God was the deity whose features the Maya regarded as being the epitome of beauty, to the extent of manipulating newborn babies' skulls to achieve a similar corncob-like shape when seen in profile. (See also pages 95 to 97.)

Like God C to his left on the bottom row of the codex page, the figure shown above (who is thought to be God R) is carrying before him a vessel contained within a net.

His unmistakably skull-like face informs the viewer that this figure on the bottom right (shown above) is God A, the death god who, it seems, bore the Mayan name Cizin (meaning "Flatulent One"). God A should not be confused with God A', who is shown at the top right of this codex page (and see detail opposite).

The Dresden Codex was damaged during the bombing of Dresden in World War II, so most reproductions seen today are based on earlier facsimiles. The reproduction of the codex page and details shown on the previous pages and at left are from a version of the codex that was first published by Ernst Förstemann in 1880. A more colorful rendition, a page from which is shown above, was published in Lord Kingsborough's 1830 work *Antiquities of Mexico*. It was hand-colored over a tracing of the Dresden Codex made during the previous decade.

Page 49 from the Dresden Codex

Thirteenth, fourteenth, or fifteenth century

Painted bark paper, Sächsische Landesbibliothek, Dresden, Germany

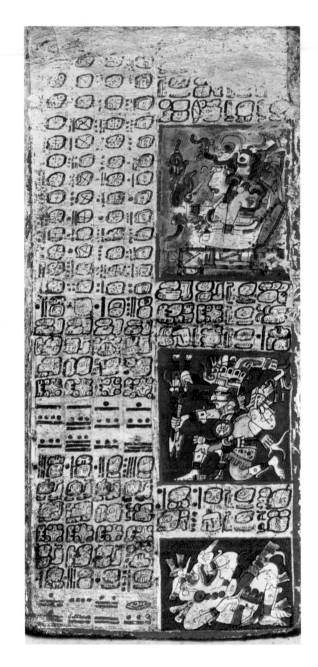

Five of the pages within the Dresden Codex are devoted to the movements of the planet Venus, which the ancient Maya believed to be a star of malevolent, drought-causing, famine-inflicting, warmongering intent and influence, and which they therefore watched both apprehensively and closely. Indeed, by calculating and recording the dates within the *tzolkin* (the 260-day calendar) on which the various phases of Venus's synodic cycle (see below) were predicted to occur, the almanac thus created could be used to ensure that earthly actions designed to limit or exploit Venus's destructive effect could be scheduled for particular days. It is thought that military engagements, for example, were planned with reference to the Venus calendar.

The page pictured at right is page 49 of the Dresden Codex (and, specifically, a reproduction of the copy made by Ernst Förstemann). This is the fourth of the five "Venus pages." The four vertical columns of glyphs on the left-hand side are concerned with Venus's 584-day synodic period, which the scribe has divided into four parts. First to be described is Venus's superior conjunction (lasting 90 days, according to this reckoning, when the planet passes behind the sun and out of sight, or, as the Maya thought, into *xibalba*, the underworld); secondly, its appearance as the Evening Star (when it rises shortly after sunset, after which the Maya believed that it followed the sun into the underworld, a phase noted here as lasting 250 days); thirdly, its inferior conjunction (when Venus passes in front of the sun, causing, as written here, 8 days of invisibility); and, fourthly, its Morning Star phase (when Venus rises before dawn, leading the Maya to believe that it guided the sun out of the underworld, a phase recorded as lasting for 236 days).

Three divinities have been pictured to the right of these columns of glyphs. The identities of the regnant deity that presides over Venus's Morning Star phase and of the victim god vary over the five Venus pages, those on page 49 being identified as the Moon Goddess (the enthroned female at the top) and the Turtle God (the prostrate figure at the bottom). And the central character, the dominant, belligerent "spearer," represents the Morning Star at the time of its heliacal rising (i.e., its first appearance), when Venus was deemed to be at its most aggressive and dangerous.

See also **Rattle in the Form of the Moon Goddess** (pages 111 to 112) and **Funerary Urn** (pages 116 to 118).

The vertical column of glyphs on the far left of the codex page (left here) relates to the Venus cycle's superior-conjunction phase in relation to the *tzolkin*. The glyph that is repeated in this column is *lamat* (which means "Venus"), the *tzolkin*'s eighth day sign.

The third column of glyphs (at right here) concerns the inferior-conjunction phase of the Venus cycle. Written to the left of the *lamat* ("Venus") glyph are the dots and bars that signified numbers to the Maya, and in this instance, the figure 8 (the three dots together adding up to 3 and the bar denoting 5).

A delicately inscribed Venus glyph, *ek'*, which also signifies "star," features in numerous positions on this page (see detail above). Venus was named by the Maya as *Noh ek'*, or "Great Star," and *Xux ek'*, "Wasp Star."

This glyph, whose form is based on a shell, represents "zero" (or "completion") in the Maya system of mathematical notation.

The bare-breasted Moon Goddess (see also pages 111 to 112) is shown in profile (right) above the two other figures, seated on a throne whose base is adorned with a sky band.

This column (at right) is dedicated to Venus's appearance as the Evening Star. The glyph that is repeated in its upper portion is the *tzolkin*'s eighteenth day sign, *edznab* ("flint," or "flint knife").

Positioned as the right-hand column, the series of glyphs shown in the detail at left is dedicated to Venus as the Morning Star; the seventeenth of the *tzolkin*'s day signs, *caban* ("earth") recurs here.

The god of the Morning Star (named as Lahun Chan in Postclassic times), who was envisaged as a divine male warrior, directs his spear downward, toward his victim.

The spear may symbolize the piercing, potentially lethal rays sent down to earth by the "Great Star."

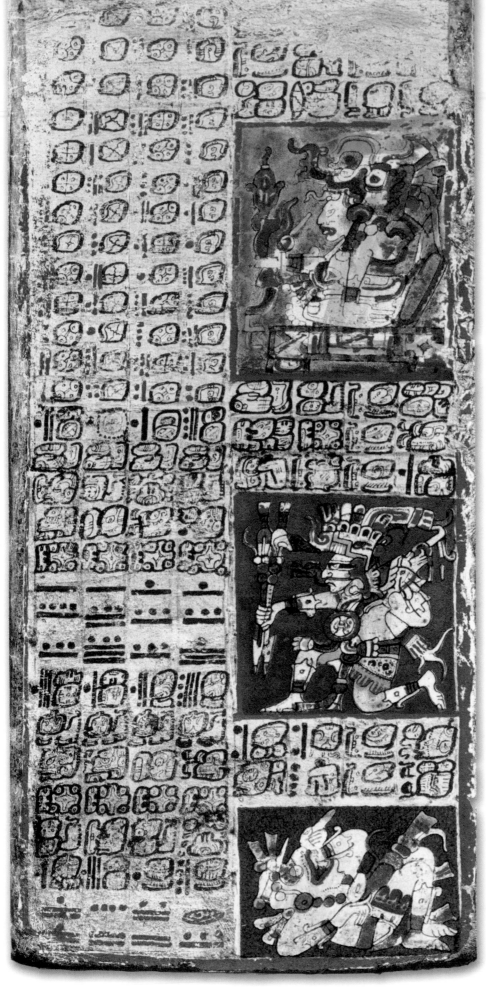

Although the Morning Star's victim has the body of a man, his head resembles that of a turtle, indicating that he is a turtle deity. The Turtle God lies prone on his back, having been speared by the Morning Star. The Maya associated the turtle with the earth, and also with the constellation of Orion.

Below, for comparison, two of the panels from the Kingsborough version of the codex, illustrating the Moon Goddess and the god of the Morning Star.

Page 74 from the Dresden Codex

Thirteenth, fourteenth, or fifteenth century

Painted bark paper, Sächsische Landesbibliothek, Dresden, Germany

Page 74 of the Dresden Codex has been widely studied in recent years by those seeking clues regarding what the ancient Maya believed would occur at the end of the Long Count that began in August 3114 BC and is scheduled to conclude in AD December 2012 (see pages 6 to 11). For the subject of this page is thought to be a cataclysmic flood unleashed upon the earth by the gods, recalling the great flood of which the Judeo–Christian Old Testament tells, as well as far more recent, localized disasters triggered by climate change. Indeed, there is a precedent for such a flood in Maya belief, for according to the *Popol Vuh* (the Quiché Maya's creation account), the male and female beings made of wood and reed that preceded humans on the face of the earth were destroyed when their divine creators, in the words of translator Allen J. Christenson, "caused the face of the earth to be darkened, and there fell a black rain, a rain that fell both day and night."

"Black sky" and "black earth" are spelled out in the glyphs at the top of the page (the reproduction shown at right is taken from the Kingsborough version, and the reproductions overleaf from the Förstemann codex; see page 63). While the representation of the rainfall may appear stylized to our eyes, there is no mistaking the torrent of water that pours from the mouth of the reptilian creature depicted in the top left-hand corner of the page—which Mayanists believe to be based on a caiman—or the two lesser streams falling from glyphs denoting eclipses hanging from the sky band to the right. The stooped figure pouring more water from a vessel has been identified as Chac Chel ("Great Rainbow"), who is in turn associated with both Ix Chel ("Lady Rainbow") and Goddess O, a deity whose areas of interest include midwifery, healing, weaving, and divination—all creative activities, suggesting that destruction and death would be followed by regeneration and rebirth, and thus maybe by a new world age. Beneath Chac Chel crouches God L (his Schellhas designation), a merchant deity with martial, underworld aspects.

See also **Foreword** (pages 6 to 11) and **Rattle in the Form of the Moon Goddess** (pages 111 to 112).

These conjoined glyphs (above) read *ik'* and *chan-na*, meaning "black sky."

This glyph is the Postclassic written form of "Chac," the name of the Maya rain god (see pages 102 to 105).

The sharp teeth visible within its long jaws and the presence of a forelimb, along with the scales that can be seen on sections of its body, all give this enormous crocodilelike creature a marked resemblance to a caiman (*Caiman crocodilus*), a water-frequenting reptile that symbolized the earth to the ancient Maya.

The caiman's body has been represented as a sky band (above). The left-hand glyph within the sky band is *ek'*, meaning "Venus," while that to its right, with a cross in the upper section, is *chan-na*, which signifies "sky."

The two glyphs positioned directly beneath the sky band represent eclipses; the *kin* glyph that is just visible at the center of the left-hand glyph's pair of "wings" symbolizes an eclipse of the sun. Eclipses were regarded with apprehension by the Maya, to whom it appeared as though heavenly bodies were being devoured.

His black coloring and large "god-eye" suggest that the belligerent figure below is God L, an identification confirmed by the large bird with spotted plumage that is balanced on his head. For this is a *muan* owl—or a screech owl (*Otus asio*)—a nocturnal bird that is often portrayed perched on God L's large hat, and that is symbolically associated with rain and clouds, along with the underworld and maize.

A serpent's coiled body can be discerned on Chac Chel's head (below), snakelike hair being a feature of this goddess. Her beaky, toothless face is another of her characteristics, an indication of her great age.

That this is a scene of destruction is emphasized by the spear that God L grasps in his right hand (he holds a staff in the other).

The Förstemann version of
this page of the Dresden
Codex—seen at right and
in all the details on this
page and opposite—renders
the colors quite differently
from the same page in the
Kingsborough version, which
is shown for comparison on
the previous page.

Water gushes
from the
earthenware
vessel gripped by
Chac Chel.

Crossed bones decorate the
skirt worn by Chac Chel,
whose feet take the form of
jaguar's claws.

Page 51 from the Madrid Codex

Sixteenth or seventeenth century

Painted bark paper, Museo de América, Madrid, Spain

The colorful combination of glyphs, dots and bars, and representations of gods shown here makes up page 51 of the Madrid Codex, which is sometimes called the Tro–Cortesianus Codex in reference to the years during which it was divided into two halves that were preserved separately in Spain. (Page 51 belonged to the Troano section prior to its reunification with the Cortesianus part during the 1880s.) Many Mayanists believe that this particular codex was created by one scribal artist from a variety of sources, and that it dates from after the Spanish Conquest.

The imagery, glyphs, and symbols that were painted onto the lime-washed bark paper of codices like this were meant to be read from left to right, and from top to bottom. And the Madrid Codex was, it seems, intended to be used as an almanac that a priest would consult in order to divine, and thus determine, the best days on which to perform certain activities and ceremonies. Some of the twenty day signs of the *tzolkin*, the 260-day Maya calendrical cycle, can be seen ranged down the left-hand side of this page, for instance, while dot-and-bar symbols denoting numbers have been positioned to the right, as have portrayals of significant deities performing ritual actions. The four cardinal directions are also accorded special significance in the Madrid Codex, and more than one glyph meaning "west" is visible here.

Although Mayanists do not fully understand all that is represented on this page, it seems certain that the black god that features so prominently is Ek Chuah (also spelled Ek'Chuwah), a Postclassic-era patron deity of merchants, travelers, and cacao who is identified as God M in the Schellhas system of names. There is, in addition, speculation that the inclusion of a fire drill may relate to the end of the fifty-two-year cycle, a theory that is based in part on the New Fire ceremony held by the Aztecs to mark the end of one Calendar Round and the start of another.

See also **Page 6 from the Dresden Codex** (pages 61 to 63) and **Censer Lid** (pages 186 to 187).

This (above) is the *ahau* ("lord") glyph, which denotes the twentieth day sign in the *tzolkin*.

It is thought that the black god depicted on this page is God M, the deity that Mayanists believe equates to Ek Chuah. *Ek* is Mayan for "black." Ek Chuah was characteristically portrayed with an exaggeratedly long nose and a large lower lip overhanging his chin.

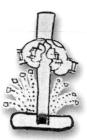

The pair of nearly identical black gods (and they are probably both portrayals of Ek Chuah) that sit facing one another in the upper section of page 51 are together using a fire drill with which to create fire by friction. And they are clearly succeeding, judging by the drill's red-hot-looking base and the sparks that are flying upward and outward to the left and right.

The footprints that are shown decorating the area on which the black gods are seated suggest that they are working on a road.

This glyph (below) spells out *chikin*, meaning "west."

The young god who is shown sitting on a throne—a symbol of his elevated status—is probably the Maize God (below). The extension of the throne back to meet what resembles a canopy above the deity's head represents a wall and ceiling (or sky band), together indicating that he is seated within a building, in all likelihood a temple.

The object that the central-section black god is wielding in his right hand (detail above) may be a rattle of a type used by the Maya in rituals and worship; alternatively, it may be a scepter.

This glyph is *edznab* (meaning "flint" or "flint knife"), which represents the eighteenth day sign in the *tzolkin*.

The oval shape and sharp point of the item that the central-section black god is clutching in his left hand tells us that it is a flint knife, which was used by the Maya both to create fire and in human sacrifice, and which could symbolize both. According to the system of mathematical notation used by the ancient Maya, three dots (each signifying 1) placed above two lines (each denoting 5) represent the number 13.

In the bottom section of the page, Ek Chuah is shown with a spear (he also had a martial aspect) and what may be a serpent scepter in his right hand.

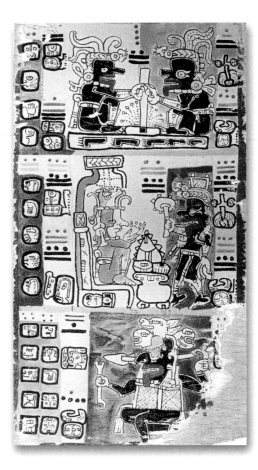

Page 10 from the Madrid Codex

Sixteenth or seventeenth century

Painted bark paper, Museo de América, Madrid, Spain

At some point between its creation and the late 1880s, the codex that we now know as the Madrid Codex was divided into two sections, respectively called the Troano Codex and the Cortesianus Codex (hence the Madrid Codex's alternative name, the Tro–Cortesianus Codex). During the period of its separation, this page—page 10—belonged to the Cortesianus Codex. Mayanists are not certain of the precise overall meaning of the glyphs, bars and dots, and divine representations that crowd it (and others), but they do have a good idea of the Madrid Codex's purpose. For the combination of day signs taken from the *tzolkin* (the 260-day calendar used by the Maya), which run in a vertical column from the top to the bottom of its pages, along with the information-providing glyphs, numerical notations, and representational imagery seen within the stacked horizontal bands to the right together indicate that the Madrid Codex was primarily an almanac. Furthermore, it was an almanac that would have been used by priests to work out the most (and least) auspicious days on which to perform certain rituals—including making placatory offerings to the gods—and their associated activities, such as sowing seeds.

The god that appears the most frequently on this page is Chac, the Maya god of rain and water, whose long, curling nose and other characteristic features make him instantly recognizable. It therefore follows that this was the deity whose influence was paramount on the days associated with page 10. And because their civilization depended on agriculture for its survival, and especially on the successful cultivation of its staple crop of maize, the Maya anyway accorded the god who, they believed, provided life-sustaining rain a prominent place in their pantheon. In addition, because the thin blue vertical lines that surround many of the characters depicted here represent rain, it is likely that this page is primarily concerned with harnessing Chac's benign influence in order to make the earth fertile and productive.

See also **Page 74 of the Dresden Codex** (pages 67 to 69) and **The Rain God Chac** (pages 102 to 105).

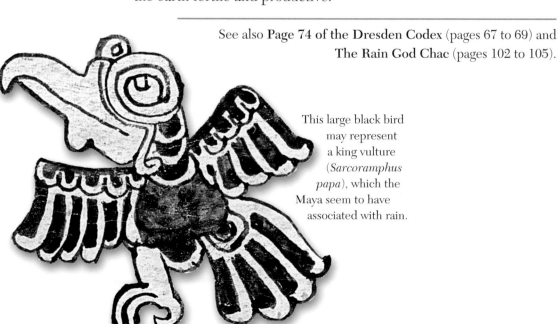

This large black bird may represent a king vulture (*Sarcoramphus papa*), which the Maya seem to have associated with rain.

A dot (signifying 1) positioned above a stack of three bars (each denoting 5) represents the number 16 in the Maya system of mathematical notation.

The number 9 is symbolized by four dots (each denoting 1) above one bar (which signifies 5).

Many of the features that distinguish Chac, according to Maya artistic convention, are visible in this portrayal of the rain god (below, right). They include an elongated, curling nose (or upper lip) that overhangs his mouth, large "goggle" eyes, and barbel-like protrusions emerging from the corners of his mouth. He may also wear ear decorations in the form of *Spondylus* (spiny-oyster) shells.

Her toothless mouth, snaking locks, hands like jaguar claws, and the skirt that she wears all suggest that this (below, right) is Goddess O, according to the Schellhas system of naming gods, an aged deity whom the Maya may have called Chac Chel (see also pages 67 to 69).

Here, Chac has been portrayed with a serpent's body, probably in a symbolic allusion to the lightning that often accompanies the rain that the Maya believed was sent to earth by the god.

The *nohol* glyph means "south."

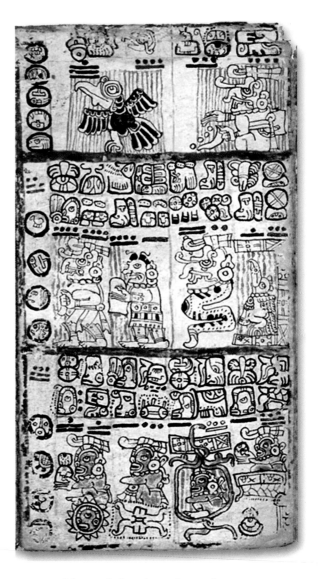

Mayanists have identified this bird (above) as a hummingbird, and its long beak bears a flowerlike mark that refers to the blooms into which hummingbirds stick their bills in search of nectar. It is shown looking upward, toward the sky (signified by a sky band), with rain streaming down around it.

Slung around the hummingbird's neck is a bag of the type that would have contained *copal*, or incense, which was used in Maya purification rituals.

Page 10 of the Madrid Codex is shown above in its entirety. The page is divided into three horizontal sections, with a row of glyphs and numerical signs running down the left-hand side in a vertical column. The day signs (three of which are picked out in details here) run down the left side of the page.

This glyph is *chuen* ("monkey"), which is the eleventh of the 260-day calendar's twenty day signs.

The *men* glyph, which symbolizes the fifteenth day sign in the 260-day calendar, means "eagle."

The twentieth day sign in the *tzolkin* is this one: *ahau* ("lord").

This is the *kuhul* glyph, which signifies "holy."

Maya scribes used three dots to represent the number 3.

Page 36 from the Madrid Codex

Sixteenth or seventeenth century

Painted bark paper, Museo de América, Madrid, Spain

Included within the pages of the Madrid Codex are sections containing instructions for celebrating the new year. And the glyphs and images that fill page 36 (which once belonged to the Troano section of the Tro–Cortesianus Codex, as the Madrid Codex is alternatively known, and which is reproduced here) are thought to focus on the *uayeb* rituals required before the start of a *muluc* year.

The Maya regulated their days using a 260-day calendar (the *tzolkin*) and a 365-day "vague-year" calendar (the *haab*), which operated in tandem. The *haab* comprised eighteen twenty-day months, which were followed by a five-day *uayeb* period, this being considered unlucky at best, and even dangerous. As a *haab* ended and a new year approached, rituals were performed during the *uayeb*, their exact nature depending on the "year-bearer" identified with the coming year, this being one of four day signs from the *tzolkin*. The year-bearers seem to have varied over time, but those in the Madrid Codex accord with the quartet of the Postclassic era: *kan* (the fourth day sign), *muluc* (the ninth), *ix* ("jaguar," the fourteenth), and *cauac* ("storm," the nineteenth).

As well as being depicted in the codices of the Maya, the *uayeb* ceremonies were described by the Spanish bishop Diego de Landa (1524–79) in his eye-witness account *Relación de las cosas de Yucatán* (*An Account of the Things of Yucatán*). From these sources, we know that offerings of food—including turkeys and maize—drink, incense, and worshipers' blood were made to ceramic "idols," or statues of the god associated with the particular year and its patron deity, and that certain dances—including war dances—were performed. At the end of the *uayeb* period, the beginning of the new year was marked, in the case of a *muluc* year, by the figure of Kinich Ahau (the sun god and patron of the year) being installed in the temple, while the year's "idol," Chac u Uayeb, was borne to the city's northern entrance and erected there. *Muluc* was associated with the north (*kan*'s direction was east, that of *ix* was west, and *cauac*'s was south), and the divine image would remain in this northerly spot for the entire year.

See also **Page 10 from the Madrid Codex** (pages 72 to 75).

This (above) is the *muluc* glyph. The ninth day sign in the *tzolkin*, the 260-day calendar, *muluc* conveys the meaning of "jade" or "water."

The tall stilts being balanced on toward the left of the page's upper section are almost certainly a reference to the stilt-dancing that we know was performed by older Maya women to end a *kan* year and usher in a *muluc* year.

A pair of disembodied blue feet (detail at left) may symbolize dancing.

This object may represent the unembroidered cloth that was an offering required before a *muluc* year.

The jaguar skin worn on the back of the figure on the right suggests that he is someone of high status, such as a king or god (see also page 60).

The presence of so many canine creatures in the lower half of page 36 may indicate the sacrifice of dogs as offerings. We know that impending *muluc* years demanded the sacrifice of a dog with a black back and that older Maya women made offerings of ceramic dogs supporting bread on their backs.

This pedestal is actually the *tun* ("drum") glyph. According to the *haab*, the 365-day calendar, 1 *tun* represents 18 *uinals*, or 360 days (1 *uinal* equaling 20 days).

This bird has been identified as an ocellated turkey (*Agriocharis ocellata*). Domesticated by the Maya, turkeys were both eaten and offered to the gods.

The flames rising from a ritual vessel suggest that this (left) is a censer within which incense is being burned.

The black bird pictured on top of an offering vessel is thought to represent a black vulture (*Catharista urubu*).

Two glyphs signifying *kan* ("maize"), the fourth of the *tzolkin*'s day signs and the year-bearer preceding *muluc*, have been piled into an offering vessel.

Front of Stela A, Copán

Stone, Copán, Honduras, Central America

Like many other Mesoamerican peoples, the ancient Maya erected stelae (stone pillars that may have evolved from trees) within their ritual centers to serve as imposing monuments that simultaneously proclaimed the power of ruling kings and commemorated the significant dates that occurred during their reigns through the sculpting of iconic portraits and the inscription of glyphs. Because these glyphs typically included a ruler's biographical details, such as the date on which he (or she) was born, ascended the throne, or won a decisive battle, they are now also regarded as invaluable historical records. And because they were set in stone, glyphs inscribed on stelae have survived in much better shape than those written on the far more destructible codices, for example. Other important events that stelae marked were landmark dates in the Maya Long Count calendar, such as the completion of a *katun* period (7200 days), which was generally celebrated with public festivities.

The images on the following pages present views of two sides of Stela A, which stands at Copán, an erstwhile eastern Maya city-state that is today part of modern-day Honduras. Copán's ruling dynasty having been established by King Yax Kuk Mo', who reigned from AD 426 until 437, Stela A was erected in 731 by one of his successors, King Waxaklahun Ubah K'awil, who is also known as King Eighteen Rabbit, or 18 Rabbit, who ruled from 695 until 738. King Eighteen Rabbit is depicted here on the eastern side (the front) of Stela A—one of a number of stelae bearing his image—his torso having been curiously compressed in its rendering, presumably to give greater prominence to the headdress, one of the most important iconographic elements of such portrayals. As illustrated by this fine example, Copán's stelae are notable for the elaborate, "baroque" style of their deep-relief carvings, which was facilitated by the trachyte (volcanic rock, or tuff) from which they were chiseled. (See pages 80 to 81 for further information on Stela A's western side.)

See also **Back of Stela A, Copán** (pages 80 to 81).

The sculptors of Copán developed a style in which the city's kings are portrayed facing the viewer.

In Stela A, King Eighteen Rabbit's serene-looking face is crowned by an ornate headdress featuring a woven-mat design (a symbol of rulership) and framed by other ritual-costume elements that, as well as being decorative, have sacred symbolic significance.

The prominent deity mask at the apex of King Eighteen Rabbit's headdress has been identified as representing a local patron god of Copán, possibly K'uy Nik Ajaw.

King Eighteen Rabbit grasps a double-headed serpent bar between his hands. Also known as a ceremonial bar, the double-headed serpent bar was a Maya symbol of kingship that may represent the sky or the Milky Way.

In holding it, the king may therefore be regarded as upholding the sky itself, thus playing a crucial role in supporting the cosmic order, as well as the gods and ancestors inhabiting the celestial realm.

Seen here in profile (right), the head that has apparently issued from the mouth of one of the snakes positioned at each end of the double-headed serpent bar appears to be that of Kinich Ahau, the sun god. The sun god is usually shown with "T"-shaped upper incisors, a roman nose, and a *kin* ("sun" or "day") sign on his forehead or cheek, which all appear to be present here.

Back of Stela A, Copán

AD 731

Stone, Copán, Honduras, Central America

The image at right is a view of the western side, or back, of Stela A, which was erected at the city-state of Copán during the reign of its thirteenth king, Waxaklahun Ubah K'awil, or, when translated into English, Eighteen Rabbit, or 18 Rabbit. King Eighteen Rabbit pursued an energetic architectural program following his accession to Copán's throne in AD 695, and this is just one of many stelae bearing his name and image that was erected in the city's Great Plaza (and see pages 78 to 79 for Stela A's eastern side—also seen below, left—on which this ruler is portrayed).

Although the meanings of the glyphs that have been inscribed into three of Stela A's four sides are not yet fully understood, Mayanists have identified some as being of great significance. These include the Emblem Glyphs of Tikal, Calakmul, and Palenque alongside that of Copán, suggesting at least that the four city-states enjoyed equal status. The name of Butz' Chan, the king who ruled Copán between 578 and 628, appears, too, along with a reference to Stela H (another Copán stela), and some scholars theorize that Stela A was erected to commemorate King Eighteen Rabbit's performance of a ritual (also referred to on Stela H) that somehow focused on the bones of Butz' Chan, Copán's eleventh ruler. Both the Long Count dedication dates of Stela H (9.14.19.5.0 4 Ahau 18 Muan, which equates to December 1, 730) and Stela A (9.14.19.8.12 12 Ahau 18 Cumku, January 30, 731) are furthermore included on Stela A, giving scholars a calendrical connection to puzzle over, along with a tantalizing insight into Maya ceremonial rituals.

In 738, King Eighteen Rabbit was captured and decapitated by King Cauac Sky of the city of Quiriguá, which had, since 653, been subservient to Copán, its neighbor in the Motagua Valley. And as if to underscore his supremacy, a stela dedicated to King Cauac Sky, which was raised at Quiriguá in 771, is the tallest such Maya monument discovered to date.

See also **Front of Stela A, Copán** (pages 78 to 79).

The Calendar Round date 4 Ahau 18 Muan appears in the second column of the second row, referring to the date on which Stela H was dedicated.

The glyph on the far right of the sixth row has been deciphered to read "bones" (*bakil*).

This glyph (above) has been identified as representing Butz' Chan, who acceded to the throne of Copán in 578 and died in 628.

This glyph (in the seventh row) means "were cut" (*susah*). The first glyph in the next column to its right signifies "bone" (*bak*).

Next to King Eighteen Rabbit's name is inscribed the Emblem Glyph that states "Holy King of Copán."

This pair of glyphs (above) spells out the name Waxaklahun Ubah K'awil: King Eighteen Rabbit. The trio of dots, each of which represents the figure 1, above a stack of three bars, which each represent 5, add up to the number 18.

GODS AND GODDESSES

So many idols did they have that their gods did not suffice them, there being no animal or reptile of which they did not make images, and these in the form of their gods and goddesses. They had idols of stone (though few in number), others more numerous of wood, but the greatest number of terra cotta.

—Diego de Landa, *Relación de las Cosas de Yucatán*, 1566 (*Yucatán Before and After the Conquest*, translation by William Gates).

As a Roman Catholic cleric, and therefore an unwavering representative of the monotheistic Christian religion, Diego de Landa disapproved of the multitude of "idols" that he discovered being worshiped in sixteenth-century Yucatán. And the Maya certainly both venerated a large pantheon of deities, many of them in the form of animals, reptiles, and birds (although in many cases, the exact connection between god and creature remains unclear), and represented them in stone, earthenware, and other materials, a number of them perishable—like wood—so that they no longer survive.

Mayanists' increasing comprehension of glyphs following the important epigraphic advances of the 1950s (see pages 38 to 41) has helped them to understand far more about the deities portrayed, or symbolized, in the four surviving codices (see, for instance, pages 61 to 63), on the ceramic vessels that were buried with the Maya, and in terra cotta, often in the form of incensarios (incense-burners). They now know, for instance, the Mayan names of an array of gods, although many are still, or alternatively, known in accordance with the alphabetical system devised by Paul Schellhas over a century ago. Originally running from God A (the death god who Mayanists now call Cizin) through God L (a merchant, underworld, and war god) and even farther down the alphabet, this list of names continued to be added to, with God A', for exam-

Above: Many Maya deities and supernatural beings took the form of creatures, their images often being sculpted in stone on sacred buildings.
Opposite: Sculpted heads representing the Feathered Serpent adorn the Pyramid of Quetzalcoatl at Teotihuacan. The Feathered Serpent was venerated as Kukulcan in Maya city-states like Chichén Itzá.

ple, being distinct from God A. Other such systems for referring to deities whose Maya identities are, or were, uncertain include the Palenque Triad, a collective name coined by Heinrich Berlin in 1963 to encompass the three gods individually known as GI, GII, and GIII. Another method of denoting a god or goddess is simply to describe his, her, or its appearance, association, or function: for instance, the Maize God, the Moon Goddess, and the Water Lily Jaguar (see pages 136 to 139).

The Feathered Serpent (or Kukulcan) is just one of the Maya deities that were absorbed from other cultures, its worship at Chichén Itzá having been introduced from Tollán (see page 19). Many representations of the Feathered Serpent were sculpted in stone at Chichén Itzá, and while figural depictions of Maya deities are crucial providers of information for Mayanists, so, too, are portraits painted in words, one of the most important written sources being the *Popol Vuh* ("Council Book"), the creation account of the Quiché Maya that was thought to have been set down during the 1550s, but is certainly far older.

Creator Gods and Old Deities

The *Popol Vuh* names the creators of the world as Heart of Sky, or Huracan (a sky god who manifests himself as three forms of lightning and may correspond to K'awil), and Gucumatz (a primeval-water-inhabiting feathered serpent who may be equated with Kukulcan). But Mayanists believe the creator deity Itzamna to have been one of the most significant Maya gods. Envisaged as ruling over the other gods (see pages 92 to 94), Itzamna (or God D) was also considered to have a priestly, or shamanic, aspect that encompassed curing, divination, and writing (which he was said to have invented). In addition, he was probably once venerated in reptilian form as the caiman Itzam Cab Ain (see pages 67 to 69), and in avian form as the Principal Bird Deity (which was in turn associated with Vucub Caquix, see pages 42 to 46).

Itzamna was one of a number of Maya gods who were depicted as being advanced in age, key visual features being their toothlessness, and consequently their fallen-in mouths. Other such aged deities include Chac Chel ("Great Rainbow"), or Goddess O, a goddess of curing and midwifery, divination and weaving, who may have been regarded as Itzamna's wife, and who may be one and the same as a goddess named Ix Chel ("Lady Rainbow," see pages 67 to 69). Another aged deity was Pauahtun (or God N), who was primarily imagined as holding the sky aloft, sometimes being portrayed in quadruplicate when performing this sky-bearing role (see pages 109 to 110).

Opposite: The detailing of a ceremonial arch at Labná, in Yucatán, is believed to have sacred significance, with the zigzag pattern running horizontally across the center denoting a serpent, and huts being represented on each side. A mask, possibly symbolizing Chac, can be seen on the upper left-hand corner.

Below Left: Like Pauahtun, certain deities were believed to act as sky-bearers, such as the bacab *portrayed here in bas-relief from a throne discovered at Palenque.*

Below, right: A carving of Itzamna from Toniná shows the aged god wearing his distinctive headdress, which incorporates an obsidian mirror. His bird's body suggests that he has been depicted in his Principal Bird Deity aspect.

Gods of the Sky

In the *Popol Vuh*, it is told that after defeating the lords of *xibalba* (the "place of fright," or underworld), the Hero Twins rose to the heavens, where they became the sun and the moon. They were not the only divinities with solar and lunar associations, however, although there is much that remains mysterious about the Maya Moon Goddess, who was sometimes represented as a young woman cradling a rabbit (a lunar symbol) while perched on a crescent moon (see page 111 to 112).

Far more is known about Kinich Ahau ("Sun-faced Lord"), the Maya god of the daytime sun, who is typically shown with a *kin* symbol (signifying "sun" or "day") marking his face, "T"-shaped upper-incisor teeth, and large eyes with marks in the corners that give him a cross-eyed look. It seems that many Maya tried to incorporate the latter two characteristics into their own appearance, filing their teeth into a "T"-shape to emulate Kinich Ahau's, and attempting to become permanently cross-eyed, as described by de Landa: "It was held as a grace to be cross-eyed, and this was artificially brought about by the mothers, who in infancy suspended a small plaster from the hair down between the eyebrows and reaching the eyes; this constantly binding, they finally became cross-eyed." (Kinich Ahau is also known as God G, and see pages 98 to 99 for his links with GIII of the Palenque Triad.)

The Maya depended on the sun to ripen their principal form of sustenance—maize—and also on rain to keep the maize crop well watered. One of their most important deities was therefore Chac, the god of rain and other forms of water, as well as of thunder and lightning, who is alternatively known to Mayanists as God B. Reflecting his various aspects, he could be portrayed wielding an ax or serpent (symbols of lightning), and with catfishlike barbels snaking from the corners of his mouth, his body furthermore often being colored blue in the codices (see also pages 72 to 75 and 102 to 105). In art, his most arresting feature, however, is his upper lip, which was depicted as being so long that it resembles a short elephant's trunk or wavy nose.

Like many other gods, representations of Chac often signal his divine status by means of enormous "god-eyes" containing spirals or other nonhuman-looking centers. "God-markings," or tattoolike symbols adorning the body or limbs, also proclaim to the viewer that the figure portrayed is a deity.

Gods of the Underworld

When Kinich Ahau, the god of the sun by day, sank below the horizon at night in the west, he was thought to be transformed into a completely different guise: that of a jaguar, a creature that hunts by night and whose golden eyes light up the darkness. It was therefore as the Jaguar God of the Underworld that the sun was believed to undertake the perilous journey through *xibalba* during the hours of darkness, when he was imagined either in entirely jaguar form, or else with a human face, albeit usually with jaguar ears and a "cruller," or twisted line, adorning his nose and eyes (see pages 116 to 118).

The Maya believed that while traveling through *xibalba*, the Jaguar God of the Underworld was in grave danger from the death lords who ruled over this dark and watery realm. Rivers of blood and pus flowed through *xibalba*, according to the *Popol Vuh*, which names some of the death gods as Flying Scab, Jaundice Demon, Skull Staff, Bloody Teeth, and Bloody Claws. Mayanists know of other death deities, too, such as God A' and God A, whose Maya name may have been Cizin, or "Flatulent One" (see pages 61 to 63). Symbols of death, such as skulls, skeletal figures, crossed bones, and eyeballs typically identify these death gods, or lords of *xibalba*, in the codices and on decorated ceramic vessels.

The Hero Twins, the Maize God, and Divine Associations

Xibalba and its death lords feature significantly in the *Popol Vuh*, and specifically in the section that concerns the story of Hun Hunahpu, and of his sons, the Hero Twins. According to the tale told, the noisy ballplaying of Hun Hunahpu and his twin brother, Vucub Hunahpu, on earth so disturbed the death lords below that they summoned the brothers to *xibalba* to compete against them. (For more on the mythical aspects of the ballgame, see pages 47 to 60.) The death lords eventually defeated and sacrificed the brothers, burying their bodies beneath Crushing Ballcourt and placing Hun Hunahpu's head in a calabash tree. There, the head magically impregnated Lady Blood, who later fled *xibalba* for the earth, where she gave birth to Hunahpu and Xbalanque: the Hero Twins. After killing Vucub Caquix, who had falsely proclaimed himself to be the sun (see pages 113 to 115), the ballplaying Hero Twins were called to *xibalba* by

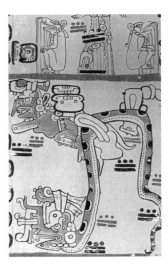

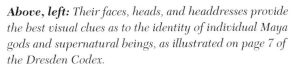

Above, left: Their faces, heads, and headdresses provide the best visual clues as to the identity of individual Maya gods and supernatural beings, as illustrated on page 7 of the Dresden Codex.

Above, center: God A, or Cizin ("Flatulent One"), is portrayed with a fleshless skull for his head on page 6 of the Dresden Codex.

Above, right: Shown sitting on a serpent, Chac is depicted with blue skin, a drooping snout, a barbel snaking from the corner of his mouth, and "goggle" eyes.

Opposite, left and right: A multitude of gods can be seen on pages 81 (left) and 94 (right) of the Madrid Codex. The black god at the top of page 81 is God M, or Ek Chuah.

Right: The Maya believed that climbing the steps leading to the top of the pyramids that they constructed brought them closer to their gods.

Below: A death god, most likely God A, and Chac, the god of rain and water, sit alongside each other on page 23 of the Madrid Codex.

Above: Maize imagery abounds in this drawing of the Tablet of the Foliated Cross, which was discovered at Palenque, notably in the "foliated cross" at the center, which is believed to represent a maize tree, a symbol of regeneration.
Opposite: Pyramidal temples, such as the "Castillo" at Chichén Itzá, pictured here, were built in an attempt to bridge the gap between the earthly and celestial realms, and thus between humans and deities.
Below: A panoramic view of Altun Ha, a ruined ancient Maya site in Belize, whose ceremonial center appears to comprise two plazas and numerous temples.

the death gods, and eventually managed to trounce them. Before ascending to the skies to become the sun and the moon, the Hero Twins honored their father, assuring Hun Hunahpu that he would be worshiped on earth.

It is not mentioned in the *Popol Vuh*, but in other Maya mythical traditions Hun Hunahpu's story continues with him emerging from the underworld and appearing on earth as the Maize God, or God E (see pages 95 to 97). As the personification of maize, their staple crop, the Maize God would anyway have been an important deity to the Maya, but because maize plants apparently die each year, yet spring to life at the start of the growing season, he also came to symbolize the concepts of rebirth and regeneration. Envisaged as being handsome, vigorous, and eternally youthful, representations of the Maize God varied slightly (Mayanists speak of the "Tonsured" or "Foliated" Maize God), but generally portrayed him bedecked with adornments of jade (an indestructible stone, whose leafy-green color symbolized growth, and thus life), with abundant tresses of hair resembling corn silk, and with an elongated head shaped like a corncob. Inspired by the Maize God, and by all that he stood for, the Maya tried to mold their newborn babies in his image—for as de Landa observed: "They also had their heads and foreheads flattened from infancy by their mothers."

Elements of the Maize God's physical characteristics are evident in the idealized portraits of élite Maya men (see, for example, pages 154 to 155). Images of Maya kings made explicit reference to other gods, too, such as the Jester God, whose representation frequently featured in their headbands (see pages 142 to 145), and K'awil (God K, or GII of the Palenque Triad, and a deity linked with fire, lightning, and royalty, see pages 106 to 108), who took the form of the Manikin Scepter in their hands (see pages 146 to 148).

Communing with the Gods

While emulating their appearance was one way in which the Maya honored their gods, hoping to win their favor, making offerings to them was another— and a crucial one, as de Landa noted with reference to Ek Chuah (or God M, the deity of travelers, merchants, and cacao, see pages 70 to 71):

Even travelers on the roads carried incense with them, and a little plate on which to burn it; and then wherever they arrived at night they erected three small stones, putting a little incense in each, and three flat stones in front of these, on which they burned incense, praying to the god they called Ekchuah that he bring them safely back home; this ceremony they performed every night until their return, unless there were some other who could do this, or even more, on their account.

Imposing, multileveled pyramidal temples were constructed to enable worshipers to become closer to the celestial realm, where deified ancestors, as well as other gods, were believed to reside, with the smoke that wafted upward when incense (*copal*, for instance) and other offerings, such as blood-splashed paper, were burned being believed

to convey the offerings directly to the deities. And if the right type of ritual offering was made by an important enough individual—a member of a royal dynasty, for example—the reward might be direct communication with a divinity through the medium of a Vision Serpent (see pages 119 to 121).

The central component of such offerings was blood, given in accordance with divine demands, as expressed by the Quiché Maya's patron god Tohil in the *Popol Vuh*: "You shall first give thanks. You shall carry out your responsibilities first by piercing your ears. You shall prick your elbows. This shall be your petition, your way of giving thanks before the face of god." Examples of such autosacrifices were described by a horrified de Landa:

At times they sacrificed their own blood, cutting all around the ears in strips which they let remain as a sign. At other times they perforated their cheeks or the lower lip; again they made cuts in parts of the body, or pierced the tongue crossways and passed stalks through, causing extreme pain; again they cut away the superfluous part of the member, leaving the flesh in the form of ears. It was this custom which led the historian of the Indies to say that they practised circumcision.

As the surviving codices make clear, in order to try to win divine approval, the Maya considered it vital that the correct rituals were performed on specific occasions, such as during the five-day *uayeb* period that preceded the new year (see pages 76 to 77). De Landa was shocked by the lengths to which the Maya were prepared to go:

But because their festivals were only to secure the goodwill of favor of their gods, or else holding them angry, they made neither more nor bloodier ones. They believed them angry whenever they were molested by pestilences, dissensions, or droughts or the like ills, and then they did not undertake to appease the demons by sacrificing animals, nor making offerings only of their food and drink, or their own blood and self-afflictions of vigils, fasts and continence; instead, forgetful of all natural piety and all law of reason they made sacrifices of human beings as easily as they did of birds.

Indeed, humans were sacrificed to the gods by the Maya in various ways, including decapitation, heart extraction, and drowning, with sacrificial victims also being thrown into the Sacred Cenote at Chichén Itzá at times of drought, for example, as an offering to Chac.

Left: Yaxchilán's famous Lintel 24, reproduced here, portrays King Shield Jaguar II and his principal wife, Lady Xok. Pictured in the process of performing an autosacrificial ritual, Lady Xok is feeding a thorn-studded rope through a hole in her tongue.
Opposite: The back of Stela F at Copán, Honduras. The carvings on the stela, which commemorates King Eighteen Rabbit, shed light on how Maya rulers venerated their gods (see also pages 78 to 81).

Cylinder Vase

AD 600–750

Earthenware, Museum of Fine Arts, Boston, Massachusetts

His facial features and headdress are just some of the clues that indicate that the enthroned figure depicted in one section of the Late Classic Period Maya ceramic cylinder vase shown opposite is Itzamna (variant spellings of which include Itsamnaj; see other depictions on pages 54 and 62), or God D, as he is called in the Schellhas naming system.

Just as his face is portrayed as betraying the signs of age, so Itzamna was regarded by the ancient Maya as one of their oldest gods. As an ancient creator deity he was senior to, and more important than, other members of the Maya pantheon, which is why he is frequently shown presiding over them. Thought to be the partner of the equally aged Ix Chel, a goddess of curing and childbirth (see pages 111 to 112), Itzamna was similarly linked with healing and medicine. He was furthermore associated with esoteric wisdom and divination (and consequently with shamans and priests), and also with writing, which he was said to have invented. Itzamna may once have been worshiped in both avian and animal form, too, on the one hand as the Principal Bird Deity, or Vucub Caquix (see page 55), and, on the other, as a caiman (see page 68), a Maya symbol of the earth.

Although the *Popol Vuh*, the creation story of the Quiché Maya, does not refer to Itzamna's presence in the underworld, *xibalba* ("place of fright"), he is sometimes depicted in the context of events described as taking place there (see also page 54). Here, for example, he is portrayed facing a skeletonized head that is most likely that of Hun Hunahpuh—or Hun Hun Ajaw, as he is also called—while the Hero Twins, Hun Hunahpu's sons, sit facing him (just out of sight in this view of the decorated drinking vessel), appealing to the supreme deity on behalf of their father.

See also **Cylindrical Vessel Depicting Ballplayers and the Journey to *Xibalba*** (pages 50 to 55).

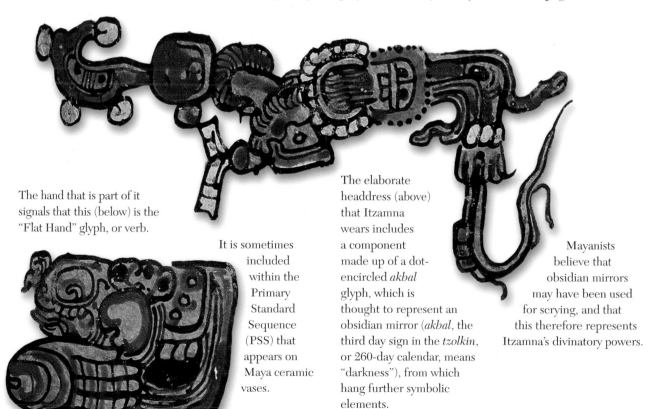

The hand that is part of it signals that this (below) is the "Flat Hand" glyph, or verb.

It is sometimes included within the Primary Standard Sequence (PSS) that appears on Maya ceramic vases.

The elaborate headdress (above) that Itzamna wears includes a component made up of a dot-encircled *akbal* glyph, which is thought to represent an obsidian mirror (*akbal*, the third day sign in the *tzolkin*, or 260-day calendar, means "darkness"), from which hang further symbolic elements.

Mayanists believe that obsidian mirrors may have been used for scrying, and that this therefore represents Itzamna's divinatory powers.

Itzamna's large, white, rectangular eye informs us that he is a god. His roman nose, as well as his sunken cheeks and toothless mouth, are all characteristic of this aged deity.

The symbol on his thigh, like the similar marks that can be seen on his back and upper arm, is a "god-marking," whose presence conveys Itzamna's divinity.

The shape and style of the patterns that can be seen on its seat and legs match those of the sky band on which Itzamna's throne stands, signifying a celestial platform and emphasizing its occupant's divine status. A segment below Itzamna's thigh comprises the *kin* glyph, which denotes the sun, or the day.

The positioning of the sky band that encircles the vase at its base, rather than along its upper rim, is deliberate, indicating as it does that the actions taking place above it are occurring in a supernatural realm, beyond the normal bounds of heaven and earth.

The "T" shape at the center of the large basket positioned in front of Itzamna's throne causes it to resemble the *ik'* glyph, which signifies "breath" or "wind," or, alternatively, "black."

Prominent among the offerings that have been piled before Itzamna is a skeletal head. This almost certainly belongs to Hun Hunahpu, the Hero Twins' father, who is also equated with the Maize God. In the *Popol Vuh*, it is told how Hun Hunahpu was decapitated in *xibalba*, his head then being placed in a calabash tree.

"The Creator of the World"

Date unknown

Earthenware, private collection

Such is its age and fragility, and the damage that this earthenware Maya artifact has suffered, that many of the details that may otherwise have helped us to deduce more about its history and meaning have been lost. Yet the iconic combination of a human figure rising above a turtle is not unusual in the art of the ancient Maya, from which we may conclude that it represents the Maize God emerging from the earth, symbolized by a turtle.

In the *Popol Vuh*, the Quiché Maya's creation story, it is related that Hun Hunahpu was summoned, along with his brother, Vucub Hunahpu, to *xibalba*, the "place of fright" or underworld, to play a ballgame against the underworld lords (see also pages 47 to 60). Here the brothers were defeated and sacrificed, their bodies then being buried beneath a ballcourt, and Hun Hunahpu's decapitated head being placed in a calabash tree. His head later having magically impregnated Lady Blood, she fled *xibalba* for the earth's surface, where she gave birth to his sons, the Hero Twins, Hunahpu and Xbalanque. When they were grown, they, too, traveled to *xibalba*, where they eventually avenged the deaths of Hun Hunahpu and Vucub Hunahpu. They then honored their father before rising to the sky as the sun and moon, leaving Hun Hunahpu's heart in the underworld ballcourt.

From their reading of other texts, many Mayanists have identified Hun Hunahpu with the Maize God, or God E in the Schellhas deity-naming system, who, with the help of his sons, was said to have been reborn from the earth, just as maize seedlings push their way out of the ground at the start of the growing season, later being harvested when ripe (and a maize ear's harvesting may be symbolically linked with Hun Hunahpu's decapitation). Both Hun Hunahpu and the Maize God are also equated with Wak-Chan-Ahaw ("Raised-up Sky Lord"), who is said to have instigated the world's creation on August 13, 3114 BC by causing the "three [hearth]stones of creation" to be positioned in the sky, these being thought to be the stars Alnitak, Saiph, and Rigel within Orion, a constellation that the Maya envisaged as a turtle. All of these divine characters are furthermore linked with the creator deity Hun-Nal-Ye, called "First Father" because, according to the *Popol Vuh* and other sources, humankind was fashioned from a dough made of maize, the staple food of the ancient Maya.

See also **Cylindrical Vessel Depicting a Ballgame** (pages 56 to 60).

The serpentine-looking head above (which may once have been balanced by another, emerging from the opposite side of the figure's headdress) may represent the double-headed serpent bar, which is in turn thought to symbolize the sky, and perhaps specifically the Milky Way, which the ancient Maya regarded as the road to *xibalba*. For each year on August 13—traditionally the date of creation—the constellation Orion (envisaged by the ancient Maya as a turtle) rises near the spot where the Milky Way crosses the ecliptic, and it may be that the ancient Maya believed that the Maize God was reborn each year on this date.

The Maize God was typically depicted as a handsome young man whose features, although regular, were somewhat elongated to suggest the shape of a corncob. (See also page 62.)

To the Maya, the aquatic turtle symbolized the earth floating on the primeval waters. Images of the resurrected Maize God often show him emerging from a fissure in a turtle's upper shell, and it is easy to see the edges of the scutes that make up a turtle's carapace as the cracks formed when earth is extremely parched.

If this figure does indeed represent the resurrected Maize God, it is particularly appropriate that it should have been modeled from clay dug from the very earth from which he was believed to have risen.

Representations of the Maize God sometimes portray him wearing jewelry, as well as a skirt, incorporating jade, a stone whose green color caused it to symbolize maize foliage and unripe maize kernels, and thus also fertility and life.

The curved elements above the figure's ears may denote long, floppy maize leaves.

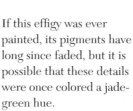

If this effigy was ever painted, its pigments have long since faded, but it is possible that these details were once colored a jade-green hue.

Maya Incense-burner

c.692

Ceramic, Museo de Palenque, Chiapas, Mexico

Although the incensario (incense-burner or censer) shown opposite was discovered within the Temple of the Sun at Palenque, and the square eyes and protruding tooth of the face staring out from it bring Kinich Ahau, the Maya sun god, to mind, certain subtle details suggest that the effigy may portray another deity. The artifact's discovery in Palenque is also significant in this respect on account of this city-state's three patron deities: GI, GII, and GIII, together known as the Palenque Triad. It is thought that the triad's individual identities may have stretched beyond Palenque, however, with GIII corresponding to Kinich Ahau (or God G), GII being equated with God K, K'awil, or the Manikin Scepter (see pages 106 to 108), and GI being a form of the rain god Chac, or Chac Xib Chac (see pages 102 to 105).

Each divine member of the Palenque Triad was linked with one of the trio of temples collectively called the "Group of the Cross," which was dedicated in AD 692 by King Kan Balam II, who ruled Palenque from 684 to 702. While GI is linked with the Temple of the Cross, GII is connected to the Temple of the Foliated Cross, and GIII is associated with the Temple of the Sun. GIII's likely divine correspondent, Kinich Ahau ("Sun-faced Lord"), was viewed by the Maya as the god of the sun by day, with the Jaguar God of the Underworld being considered the deity of the night-time sun (see pages 116 to 118), and it is unmistakably portrayals of the latter that figure prominently in the Temple of the Sun. The features that generally identify Kinich Ahau (and GIII) are "T"-shaped upper-incisor teeth; a roman nose; barbels snaking from the corners of his mouth; rectangular eyes with crossed pupils; and a *kin* ("sun" or "day") sign on his forehead or body. Depictions of GI, by comparison, typically include a single shark's tooth emerging from beneath his upper lip; barbels protruding over his lower lip; *Spondylus*-shell (spiny-oyster-shell) ear decorations; and "god-eyes" enclosing spirals. Taking these characteristics into consideration, it seems most likely that the deity depicted at the center of this incense-burner is GI.

See also **Maya Incense-burner depicting a Maya noble** (pages 100 to 101).

This slightly curved protrusion may represent a flame, perhaps a visual reference to the incensario's function, which was to support braziers in which offerings of incense were burned.

A pair of closed eyes draws the viewer's attention to what appears to be a mask (below) positioned above the god's head.

The paint that described it has faded with age, but it appears as though this exaggeratedly large "god-eye" (below) once bore a spiral pattern, a hallmark of GI of the Palenque Triad.

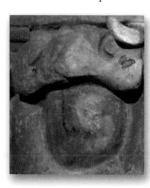

The long, curving form at the center of this decorative side section (above) may indicate a serpent's body.

It is possible that the spiked circular shapes directly above the god's ears represent spiny-oyster (*Spondylus*) shells.

 Diagonal crosses like this are often seen within sky bands in Maya art, and may signify a celestial event, such as a conjunction.

It may look like a tongue, but the object that protrudes from the god's open mouth is actually a tooth. While representations of Kinich Ahau are notable for their "T"-shaped upper incisors, GI is often shown with a pointed shark's tooth similar to this. (It seems that the early morning sun was sometimes envisaged as a shark by the Maya.)

 Barbels extend from each side of the central face's lower lip.

The paired flowerlike devices depicted on either side of the god's chin denote ear flares. Traces of the original turquoise color used for decoration remain strong here.

The incense-burners of Palenque are notable for their stacked style, in which masks appear one above the other. Another pair of eyes at the base of the censer indicates that this area comprises the lowest of the incensario's tiered masks.

Maya Incense-burner

c.692

Ceramic, Museo de Palenque, Chiapas, Mexico

The incensarios (censers, or incense-burners) that were discovered at Palenque, and specifically at the three temples that are collectively called the "Group of the Cross," are famous for their complex, "stacked" style, in which all manner of masks and faces appear to have been positioned on top of one another. Some of the principal heads that gaze out at the viewer amid portrayals of supernatural creatures are those of gods, such as GI of the Palenque Triad, who is seen on the incensario pictured on pages 98 to 99. The incense-burner shown opposite has a number of decorative components in common with that example, and, indeed, both come from the Temple of the Sun, and were probably manufactured in Palenque, or thereabouts, too. It is thought that these incensarios would have supported braziers or bowls containing *copal* (incense derived from the resin of Bursera trees) and paper soaked with blood produced by autosacrifice, which would have been lit for purification and offering rituals. Mayanists believe that these incensarios—called "god censers" (*p'ulut k'u*) in Palenque—were used for an entire *katun* (a Long Count period equating to 7200 days, or nearly 20 years) before being retired from service and interred.

We do not know the identity of the composed-looking human face that is the main feature of this incensario, but he is unlikely to be a member of the Maya pantheon, and more likely to be a deified ancestor from Palenque's ruling dynasty. (The Temple of the Cross, the Temple of the Foliated Cross, and the Temple of the Sun—the "Group of the Cross"—were all dedicated in AD 692 by Kan Balam II, Palenque's king from 684 until 702, and the son of the great King Pacal, who reigned from 615 to 683.)

The Maya believed that long-dead divine ancestors could be conjured up amid the copious clouds of smoke yielded by the burning of *copal*, when they would emerge from the mouth of a Vision Serpent to appear before their descendants in the earthly realm (see pages 119 to 121).

See also **Maya Incense-burner depicting God GI** (pages 98 to 99).

The triangular object that hangs from the left hand of the spectacularly crowned man who sits cross-legged at the apex of the incensario may denote a bag containing *copal* incense, which was believed to have purifying powers.

Bearing in mind that this artifact was used for the ritual burning of incense, Mayanists think that the two small, irregular shapes extending from each side of the incensario signify flames.

Palenque's incense-burners are characterized by their tiered, masklike components. Here, a pair of distinctly nonhuman-looking eyes can be seen staring out from between two diadems.

Diagonal crosses flank the human face that dominates the incensario. Crosses like these are often seen in sky bands, and may symbolize celestial conjunctions.

The youthful, symmetrical, and serene male face has been portrayed in accordance with the Maya ideal of beauty, which was based on representations of the Maize God.

Although little remains of the paint that once gave detail to the man's eyes, traces of his dark irises can still be seen.

The man's striking pair of three-dimensional ear decorations remains intact. Flowerlike ear flares have also been incorporated into the decorative elements on either side of his face.

A necklace made up of large painted beads displays a human head as its centerpiece.

A rectangular-shaped pair of eyes has been positioned at the bottom of the stack of masks.

The Rain God Chac

Sixteenth or seventeenth century

Painted bark paper, British Museum, London

Chac, the Maya god of rain and water, and of thunder and lightning, dominates all four "quarters" of the image shown at right, which comprises pages 3 (the left-hand half) and 4 (the right-hand half) of the Madrid Codex, or the Tro-Cortesianus Codex (and during the period of the codex's division into two, these pages belonged to the Cortesianus section). Along with the Maize God, this deity—of which God B of the Schellhas naming system is considered a form—was one of the most significant members of the Maya pantheon, also being among the longest worshiped. Indeed, he is still invoked today in the Yucatán when rain is urgently desired.

The main reason why Chac was so fervently venerated was because it was he who, it was believed, sent the life-giving rain from the skies without which no human being, bird, or beast could survive, no fish could thrive, and no maize (the staple crop of the Maya) could grow, so that a prolonged absence of rain meant drought and death. He was not regarded as being entirely benevolent, however. He was feared on account of the destructive thunderstorms that he unleashed on the earth below, and he was often depicted holding a serpent or an ax in his hand, both of which symbolized thunderbolts. Portrayals of Chac in codices and other Maya art forms are relatively easy to identify: often tinted blue (to signify rain-water), the rain god is typically shown with a human or serpentine body, the latter symbolically referring to water and lightning. His head is especially distinctive, featuring as it does a long, pendulous snout that resembles a short elephant's trunk; "goggle" eyes; barbels, or tendrils, which may be depicted as snakes, emerging from the corners of this mouth; large ear ornaments, often in the form of *Spondylus* (spiny-oyster) shells; and a hank of hair tied on top of his head.

See also **Page 10 from the Madrid Codex** (pages 72 to 75).

The glyph that appears twice to Chac's left is *edznab*, which means "flint," or "flint knife." This is the eighteenth day sign in the *tzolkin*, the 260-day calendar used by the Maya.

The flaming torch that Chac carries before him represents a thunderstorm, and especially the fire that may be ignited by lightning bolts.

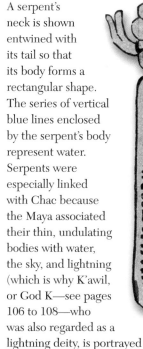

According to the Maya system of mathematical notation, three dots (each of which signify 1) above three bars (a bar denotes 5) together symbolize the number 18.

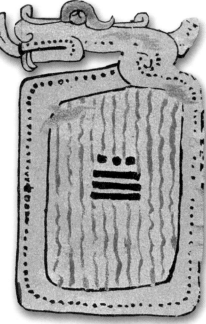

A serpent's neck is shown entwined with its tail so that its body forms a rectangular shape. The series of vertical blue lines enclosed by the serpent's body represent water. Serpents were especially linked with Chac because the Maya associated their thin, undulating bodies with water, the sky, and lightning (which is why K'awil, or God K—see pages 106 to 108—who was also regarded as a lightning deity, is portrayed with a snake foot).

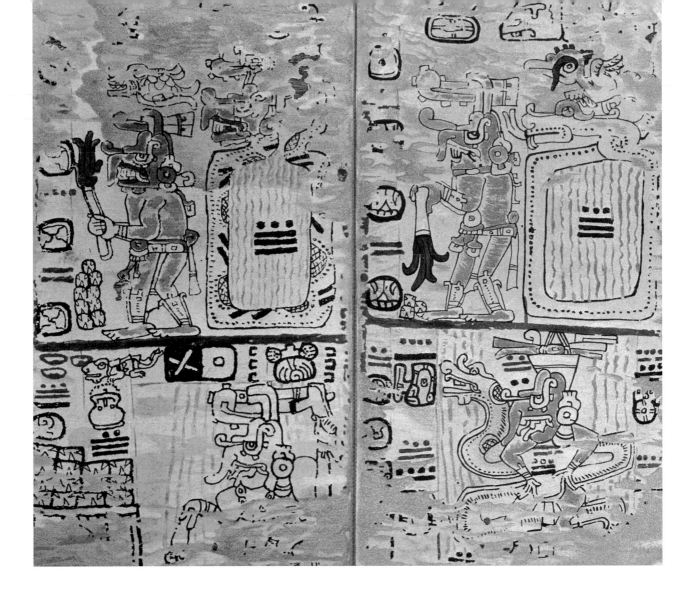

Chuen ("monkey"), the *tzolkin's* eleventh day sign, has been written twice to the left of Chac's upended torch.

The glyph to the right of Chac's head spells *nohol*, meaning "south."

The creature above (lower left quarter of the image) has been identified as an iguana, a reptile that the Maya used for offerings.

Chac's skin has been colored blue in order to symbolize water.

The bird perched on top of the serpent's head and neck is an ocellated turkey (*Agriocharis ocellata*). Native to the Maya region, the turkey—which was domesticated—was regarded as a source of food.

Chac's long, drooping nose identifies the rain god. The barbel protruding from the corner of his mouth and a large, "goggle" eye are also prominent.

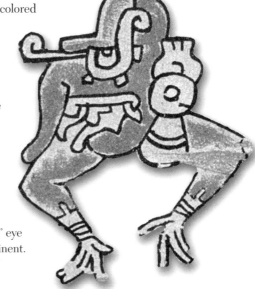

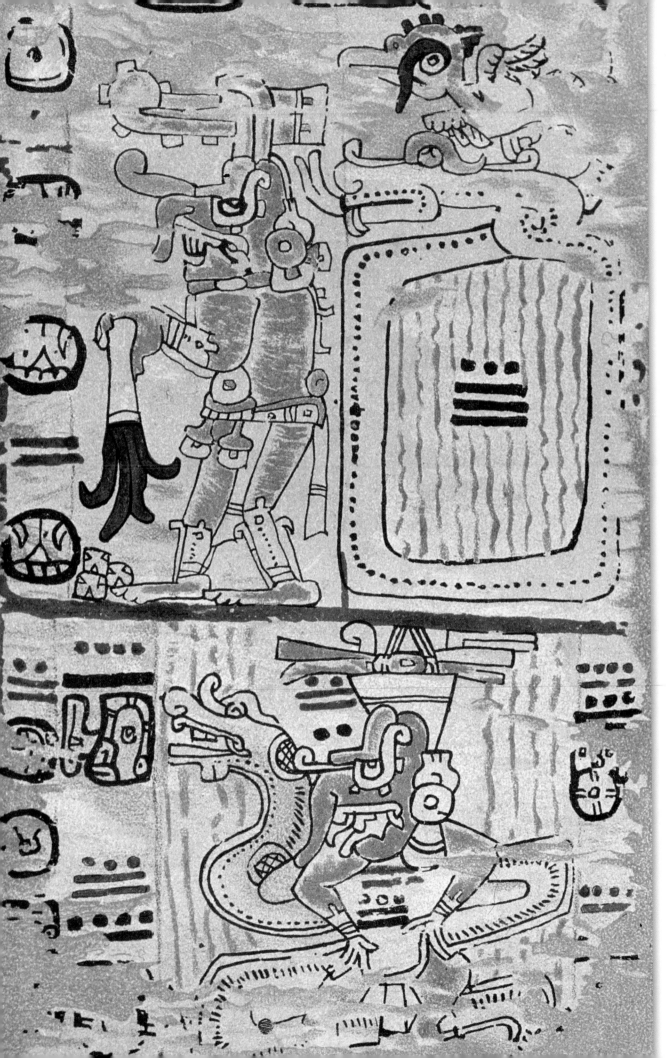

Cylindrical Vessel Depicting God K

Date unknown

Earthenware, American Museum of Natural History, New York, New York

As well as being breathtaking testaments to the artistry of those who created them, the glyphs and scenes painted on many Maya ceramics also provide us with a fascinating insight into the culture and beliefs of a lost civilization. The skill of the potter and scribal artist who made the polychrome vessel pictured here is evident, but when you consider that it was created before the arrival in Mesoamerica of the potter's wheel, and without the benefits of glaze, it reveals an extraordinary level of expertise. And because so many exquisite examples have been excavated from the tombs of high-status individuals, we can also conclude that such vessels were valued within Maya society, too. Furthermore, because some display sacred subject matter, it may be that they had a ritual function, or that they were intended to perform a supernatural service in the afterlife for the tomb-owner with whom they were buried.

The dynamic-looking being depicted in the detail seen here has been variously identified as God K (according to the nineteenth-century Schellhas system of nomenclature); GII of the Palenque Triad; K'awil (or Kauil and other variants on the name); or the Manikin Scepter, that is, when he is represented as being held, in snake-footed, miniature form, by the rain god Chac or else a Maya ruler. An ancient and important member of the Maya pantheon, it seems that God K was associated with fire and lightning (which is why he is often pictured in association with Chac), with royalty (hence his appearance in stylized, scepter form as a symbol of legitimate rulership), and with transformational energy. And it may be that the key to decoding the significance of this vessel lies in God K's transcendental, transformational power, which a tomb-owner may have wished to call upon for help as he as passed through the perilous underworld.

God K also appears on the opposite side of this cylindrical vessel, the pair of portrayals being separated by two brown-framed columns of glyphs whose edges define the vase's sides in this view.

See also **Lintel 53, Yaxchilán** (pages 146 to 148).

His elongated, upward-turning snout (which may hint at a serpentine origin), large "god-eye," and the scrolling plumes of fire and smoke that are shown emerging from his forehead are all features that signify God K.

A mirror, often smoking, positioned on his forehead is another of this deity's characteristics—and may even be included here—and this may sometimes have the blade of an ax (a lightning symbol) embedded within it.

Known as "god-markings," the tattoolike designs that are visible on God K's biceps and thigh proclaim his divine status.

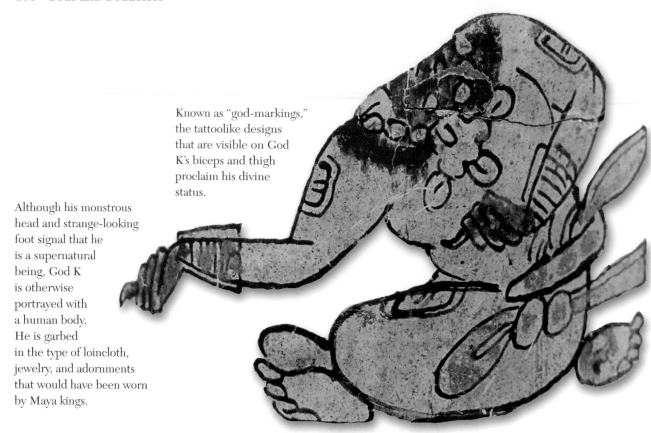

Although his monstrous head and strange-looking foot signal that he is a supernatural being, God K is otherwise portrayed with a human body. He is garbed in the type of loincloth, jewelry, and adornments that would have been worn by Maya kings.

The foot that rests in front of God K's body seems to be far larger than the one that can be seen behind him, also appearing to have a exaggeratedly enlarged big toe. This may represent the one snake-headed foot that is an unmistakable feature of the Manikin Scepter (the other is conventionally human in appearance), while the red clay-slip detailing that is shown to its left suggests flames.

The raised throne on which God K sits is a clear illustration of his elevated status as a powerful deity. And because the power of transformation with which he was credited caused the Maya to believe that he lived within temples, this throne may allude to his presence within such a sacred setting.

The circle-within-a-cross motif between the throne's legs is not merely decorative, recalling as it does the *k'an* glyph that conveys such concepts as the color yellow, preciousness, and the south. It is not certain exactly what the glyph means in this context, but it is thought to have astronomical significance, and may allude to a conjunction of planets.

Polychrome Two-part Effigy Vessel Early Classic Period

Pottery, Museo Arqueológico de Tikal "Sylvanus Griswold Morley," Tikal, Petén, Guatemala

King Yax Nuun Ayiin I—who is also called Nuun Yax Ayiin, or, in English, Curl Snout or Curl Nose—was the ruler of the city-state of Tikal, in the Petén area of Guatemala, from AD 379 to around 404. When he died, his body was entombed in Tikal's North Acropolis (and Mayanists refer to his grave as Burial 10 in Temple, or Structure, 34), as was the striking-looking effigy vessel shown below. Consisting as it does of two parts, it is likely that the intention was for incense to be burned within the vessel—although if it was indeed a censer, or incensario, it appears never to have been used—or else that it was created to serve as a container for a more substantial offering.

The effigy into which this polychrome pottery vessel has been fashioned represents an elderly-looking deity balancing a human head in his cupped hands. This may be the Central Mexican deity known as the Old God, but has also been identified as the Maya God N, who is additionally named as Pauahtun (or Pawahtuun). This divinity is generally depicted with lined and sunken cheeks, and with teeth that are few and far between (and sometimes also with outsized "god-eyes"), as well as with a roman nose, a netlike headdress, and occasionally a conch or turtle shell on his back, from which he may alternatively be shown emerging. Despite being regarded as a skybearer (and when performing this role, he may be depicted in quadruplicate, with each Pauahtun supporting one of the four quarters of the universe), this god was also linked by the ancient Maya with thunder, mountains, and the earth's interior, and thus with the underworld. This made him an appropriate choice of deity for an effigy vessel that, it was thought, would accompany the king to the underworld after his death (see also pages 188 to 189). Pauahtun was additionally considered a patron of scribes, and was furthermore believed to oversee the ending of the old year. (See also pages 92 to 94 for details of another old Maya god: Itzamna.)

See also **Cylinder Vase** (pages 92 to 94).

It is thought that this hollow projection was designed to enable smoke to escape from the vessel when a flame was lit within it, maybe in order to burn incense.

His large, circular earrings are a sign of this aged god's high status.

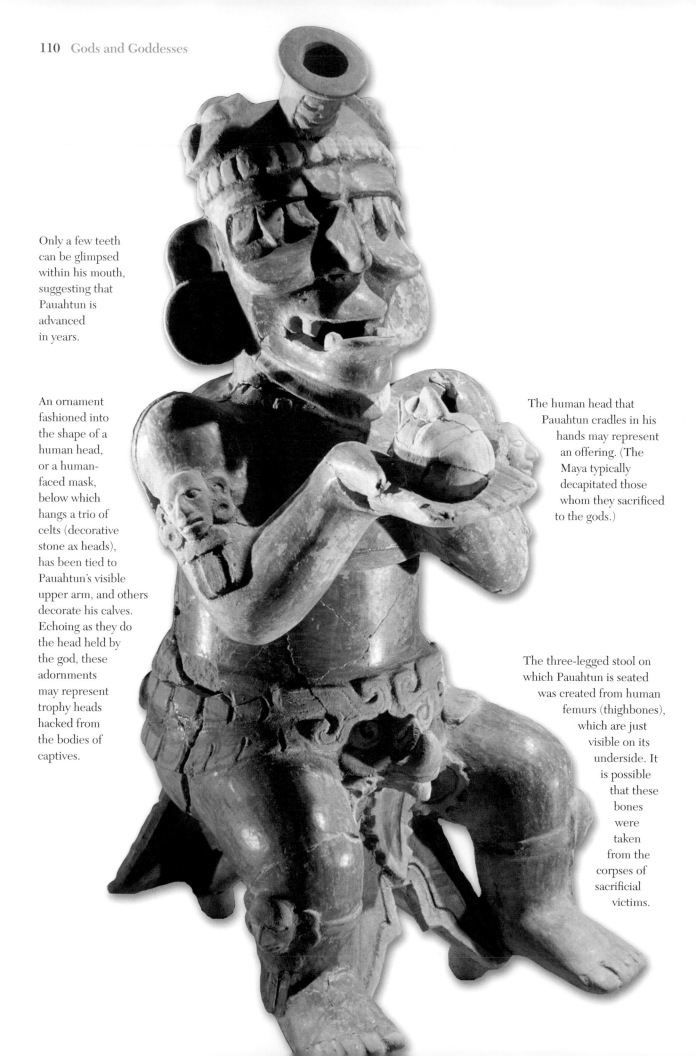

Only a few teeth can be glimpsed within his mouth, suggesting that Pauahtun is advanced in years.

An ornament fashioned into the shape of a human head, or a human-faced mask, below which hangs a trio of celts (decorative stone ax heads), has been tied to Pauahtun's visible upper arm, and others decorate his calves. Echoing as they do the head held by the god, these adornments may represent trophy heads hacked from the bodies of captives.

The human head that Pauahtun cradles in his hands may represent an offering. (The Maya typically decapitated those whom they sacrificed to the gods.)

The three-legged stool on which Pauahtun is seated was created from human femurs (thighbones), which are just visible on its underside. It is possible that these bones were taken from the corpses of sacrificial victims.

Rattle in the Form of the Moon Goddess AD 600–900

Pottery and pigment, Lowe Art Museum, Miami, Florida

It may be only a small island, but Jaina (which is situated off the coast of Campeche, to the west of the Yucatán Peninsula) is of enormous importance to Mayanists on account of the significant number of Late Classic Period burials that have been discovered there. Perhaps the most significant grave goods found on Jaina are the fired-clay figures that were buried alongside the bodies of the deceased, which have provided an invaluable insight into the clothing and costumes worn during this period—by high-status Maya individuals, as well as by ballplayers, priests, warriors, and numerous other members of Maya society, young and old, male and female. Some are thought to have been modeled on those with whom they were buried; others, like this example, depicted Maya deities. This figure is also one of many created from molds to serve as hollow rattles (or whistles), clay pellets providing the rattling sound. Jaina may have been selected as a large-scale burial site partly on account of its westerly position, and partly because it is an island. The underworld, *xibalba*, was believed to lie under water, in the direction of the setting sun, which, it was thought, descended there at night. And because the moon shines in the dark night sky after sunset, it may be that this Moon Goddess rattle was shaken as part of a burial ritual, or that it was intended for use in the afterlife.

Uncertainty clouds the name and exact nature of the Maya Moon Goddess—further confused by the *Popol Vuh*'s description of the Hero Twins rising from *xibalba* to become the sun and moon. She is often depicted in Maya art as a young and beautiful woman sitting on the curve of a crescent-shaped waxing moon holding a rabbit, a creature whose form the Maya still say they see in the face of the full moon. Identified by some with Ix Chel, an aged goddess associated with curing, childbirth, and weaving (who is in turn linked with Chac Chel and Goddess O), or with the youthful Goddess I, it now seems as though the Maya considered the young Moon Goddess a separate deity. Crescent- and full-moon decorative elements can be discerned in this figure, which portrays a good-looking Maya woman dressed in the lavish jewelry and costly garments that would have been worn by elite female Maya.

See also **Page 10, Madrid Codex** (pages 72 to 75).

The holes that can be seen above the Moon Goddess's arms are a feature of this hollow rattle's construction.

A floor-length cloak (a prestigious garment) falls from the Moon Goddess's shoulders.

The circular object whose handle the figure is clutching in her left hand may represent a tassel-decorated fan (see also page 58), or maybe a hand mirror. Either way, its shape is reminiscent of the full moon.

One of the primary symbols associated with the Maya Moon Goddess is a crescent moon, and it may therefore be that the inclusion of this crescent shape within the design of her clothing was intended to signify her lunar links.

Reflecting the garb of Maya women of the period, the Moon Goddess wears a long skirt or *huipil*, a shiftlike garment.

The figure's feet are disproportionately large in comparison with her hands. This has less to do with how the Maya envisaged the appearance of the Moon Goddess than with providing a stable "platform" on which the rattle would be able to remain balanced and erect when placed in a standing position.

The Moon Goddess's elaborate headdress and hairstyle have been finely modeled and, like many Jaina figures, bear traces of the bright-blue pigment with which they were originally painted.

Vase with Two Blowgunners and Waterbirds

AD 500–800

Earthenware with polychrome slip on painting, Museum of Fine Arts, Houston, Texas

The view of the richly colored Late Classic Period ceramic vessel seen at right may show only part of the scene that was painted around its sides, yet it conveys the high quality of the workmanship that went into making the vase itself. "Rollout" photographs, such as those on pages 50 to 55 and 56 to 60, by contrast, present panoramic scenes, but not a sense of the overall appearance, or solidity, of the artifacts that they adorn.

The section of the vase that is visible here shows a hunter crouching behind two long-billed waterbirds, having just fired a pellet from his blowgun. When the vessel is turned to the left, his target hoves into view, this being an enormous waterbird that is gripping a fish in its beak. Turn the vase to the right, and a similar-looking hunter is revealed—albeit with a bird adorning his sombrero and a face that is white, rather than black—along with more waterfowl, one of which has just been struck in the neck by a pellet from the second hunter's blowgun.

It is thought that these two huntsmen represent Hunahpu and Xbalanque, the Hero Twins whose exploits, and eventual victory over the death gods of the underworld (*xibalba*, or "place of fright"), are recounted in the *Popol Vuh*, the creation story of the Quiché Maya. Here, it is told of their skill with the blowgun: how Hunahpu shot down Vucub Caquix, or 7 Macaw, from a nance tree by hitting him in the jaw (see pages 50 to 55); how the twins went hunting daily, bringing back birds for their grandmother and brothers, Hun Batz (or 1 Batz) and Hun Chouen (1 Chouen), to eat; and how they hid within their blowguns in the House of Bats in *xibalba*, a strategy that kept them safe until Hunahpu stuck out his head and was decapitated. Yet the clever and resourceful twins managed to overcome even this significant setback, outwitting the *xibalban* lords and, according to Maya myth, resurrecting their father, Hun Hunahpu (or 1 Hunahpu, who is equated with the Maize God), before ascending to the heavens as the sun and the moon.

See also **Cylindrical Vessel Depicting Ballplayers and the Journey to *Xibalba*** (pages 50 to 55).

The high-crowned, broad-brimmed hat that the squatting figure is wearing is a sombrero.

This headgear denoted a hunter to the Maya.

Both of the figures that appear on this vase have been portrayed with black, dot-ringed circles all over their bodies. These may represent camouflage applied to disguise the hunters from their prey. They may alternatively be "god-markings," which, in Maya art, mark characters out as being supernatural beings rather than humans. In other depictions, Hunahpu's body may be distinguished by black spots, and Xbalanque's, with jaguar-skin patches.

Still gripping his blowgun firmly, the hunter has just sent a pellet flying toward his prey: a large bird that is just out of sight in this image. Maya blowgun pellets were generally made of hardened clay.

The hunter appears to have a short, neat beard, a feature that sometimes identifies Xbalanque.

This bird, as well as the others depicted alongside it on the vase, has been identified as a heron.

Incense-burner from Funerary Urn from Tapijulapa, Tabasco
Date unknown

Terra cotta, Museo Regional de Antropologia Carlos Pellicer Cámara, Tabasco, Villahermosa, Mexico

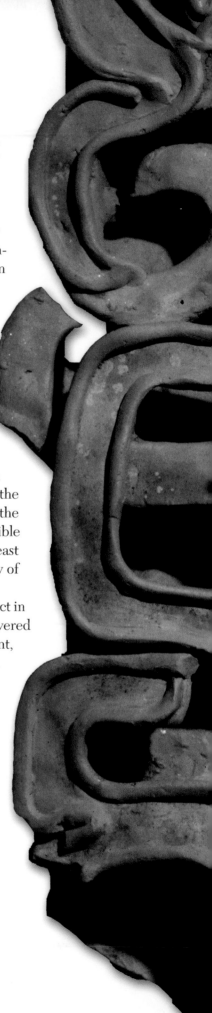

The distinctive cruller that we can see snaking from temple to temple under its eyes and over its nose informs us that the figure portrayed at the center of this terra-cotta Maya funerary urn (or, more specifically, the base of an incensario, or incense-burner, used in sacred rituals) is the Jaguar God of the Underworld. This deity is associated with the night and darkness, and also with war, the number 7, and the city of Tikal, of which he was the divine patron. Much as the lion has traditionally been considered the king of the beasts in Europe, so the jaguar (*Panthera onca*), a powerful predator that prowls the rainforests, has been feared and revered as the Mesoamerican "top cat" from at least the time of the Olmec. And it may have been the jaguar's nocturnal hunting habits and darkness-illuminating, golden-glowing eyes that led it to be considered the sun's night-time aspect.

The Maya believed that when the sun—which they identified as the god Kinich Ahau ("Sun-faced Lord") by day—sank below the horizon each night in the west, it began its journey through the underworld realms in the form of the Jaguar God of the Underworld. Here, the divine nocturnal embodiment of the sun was confronted by the horrific lords of *xibalba* ("place of fright"), the terrible underworld envisaged by the Maya. Its emergence at dawn each day in the east signaled that the sun had once again survived its nightly ordeal, but in the view of the Maya, it was by no means certain that it would always do so.

A number of the Maya incense-burners that are displayed alongside this artifact in Villahermosa, Mexico, came from Tapijulapa, Tabasco, where they were discovered in a cave that was clearly considered to be a sacred space. Indeed, it is significant, in the context of the Jaguar God of the Underworld, that caves were believed by the Maya to be entrances to *xibalba*.

See also **Maya Lord in Cacaxtla** (pages 152 to 153).

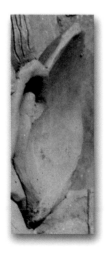

Not only does the long, pointed ear to the right of the god's headdress resemble an animal's, but it is also set on top of the deity's head, like a jaguar's ears.

Although envisaged as essentially a big cat, the Jaguar God of the Underworld is often depicted with a human face, perhaps to emphasize his supernatural status.

Jaguar features aside, the Jaguar God of the Underworld's most striking feature is the cruller, the twisted line here seen looping above the bridge of his nose and under his eyes, so called because it resembles the traditional, twisted, deep-fried cake of the same name.

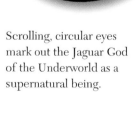

Scrolling, circular eyes mark out the Jaguar God of the Underworld as a supernatural being.

When it appears as a glyph, the cross at the center of the god's body may signify such concepts as conjunction, union, or meeting.

It may be no coincidence that this curving detail on the flange resembles a Maya glyph signifying the planet Venus.

The Maya believed that this planet led the sun out of the underworld at daybreak as the "Morning Star," and that it followed it into the underworld as the "Evening Star" at nightfall (see also pages 64 to 66).

Lintel 25, Yaxchilán

AD 726

Limestone, British Museum, London

The carved limestone lintels discovered at the erstwhile city-state of Yaxchilán, which is now in Chiapas, Mexico, have long been acclaimed as some of the finest examples of Maya sculptural art. Lintels 24, 25, and 26 are considered especially important, as much for their subject matter as for the artistry that went into their creation. Originally set above doorways within Structure, or Temple, 23 in AD 726, during the reign (from 681 to 742) of Itzaam (or Itzammaaj) Balam II—the king known to Mayanists as Shield Jaguar II—two of these lintels depict his principal wife, Lady K'abal Xok, or Lady Xok, initially engaged in bloodletting (Lintel 24) and then, as shown here, communing with the ancestral spirit that she has conjured up by her autosacrifice through the catalyst of the Vision Serpent. Although Shield Jaguar's name appears among the accompanying glyphs, it seems that the warrior portrayed between the Vision Serpent's jaws may instead be King Yat Balam (or Jaguar Penis), the fourth-century founder of Shield Jaguar's dynasty.

The ancient Maya believed that the members of their royal families were able to communicate with deified ancestors and other gods (and, indeed, that it was their duty to do so in order to enlist divine favor on behalf of their dynasty and subjects), but at a painful price. For the ecstatic trance that apparently enabled these privileged men and women to make contact with the divine realm was achieved mainly by autosacrifice, or the letting of one's own blood, as an offering to the deities, possibly aided by fast-ing, dancing, and the use of hallu-cinogens. When enough blood had flowed, the paper into which it had soaked was lit, carrying the essence of the offering to the gods, and maybe also prompting the appear-ance of a Vision Serpent within the undulating curls of smoke. The coils that comprised the bodies of such Vision Serpents (which were often depicted as double-headed creatures) were thought to act as a conduit between the divine and mortal realms, so that in this case, for instance, Yat Balam would have traveled from the super-natural sphere through the Vision Serpent's body to emerge from its jaws to appear before Lady Xok. Some Vision Serpents had specific identities, and the one that Lady Xok has conjured up here may be Waxaklahun Ubah Kan, which is also known as the War Serpent.

See also **Lintel 53, Yaxchilán** (pages 146 to 148).

Unusually, the glyphs that have been incised into Lintel 25 were written back to front. The Calendar Round date 5 Imix 4 Mac begins the inscription (*imix* being the first day sign in the *tzolkin*, or 260-day calendar, and *mac*, the thirteenth month of the *haab*, or 365-day calendar).

The central section of the text informs us that a vision has been conjured up.

The vessel by Lady Xok's feet has been filled with strips of bark paper soaked in her blood, along with the thorn-studded cord that she pulled through a hole in her tongue in order to cause it to flow, and maybe also an obsidian-bladed bloodletting tool. The contents of the bowl having been set alight, smoke now wafts and coils upward, taking the sinuous form of a Vision Serpent as it rises.

This detail (above) spells out the name Itzaam Balam, or "Shield Jaguar."

Scales emphasize that the sinuous form on the left of the image is a snake's body.

Lady Xok wears a richly decorated costume. The quatrefoil motifs on her robe are reminiscent of the *kin* ("sun") glyph and may signify her royal status.

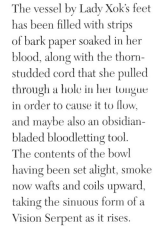

Having materialized from the portal of the Vision Serpent's (or War Serpent's) jaws, Yat Balam looks down at Lady Xok. He holds a round shield in his left hand and a flint-tipped spear or lance in his right.

This glyph (above) gives the queen's name: Na K'abal Xok (Lady K'abal Xok).

Lady Xok balances a bowl on the palm of her left hand. Like the vessel positioned in front of her, it contains paper strips spattered with blood from her wounded tongue, as well as instruments of bloodletting.

It is difficult to discern, but the skeletal head of a war god has emerged from the Vision Serpent's second head. The same "balloon" headdress as that worn by Yat Balam at the opposite end of its body is, however, easy to spot.

Possibly weakened by pain and blood loss, Lady Xok (right) is clearly in a trancelike state as she gazes up at the ancestral vision that she has conjured up.

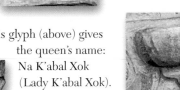

LIFE AND DEATH

The Indian women raised their children both harshly and wholly naked. Four or five days after the child was born they laid it on a small cot made of rods, face down, with the head between two pieces of wood, one on the occiput and the other on the forehead, tying them tightly, and leaving it suffering for several days until the head, thus squeezed, became permanently flattened, as is their custom. This however caused so great distress and risk for the poor infants that they were at times in danger of death; and the author hereof saw one where the head was pressed back of the ears, which must have happened to many.

—Diego de Landa, *Relación de las Cosas de Yucatán*, 1566 (*Yucatán Before and After the Conquest*, translation by William Gates).

Above: Looking at this detail, it is easy to see why the style of architecture seen at Copán is often described as "baroque." Although decorative, such details also had cosmic and sacred symbolic significance.
Opposite: A portrait in stone of King Pacal of Palenque illustrates the idealized appearance that was prized by the Maya. Modeled on images of the Maize God, the tapering head shape seen here was achieved by squashing newborn babies' skulls between planks of wood.

Writing in 1566 of his experiences in the Yucatán Peninsula, the Spanish Roman Catholic cleric Diego de Landa expressed his disgust at the seemingly cruel head-shaping practice to which the Maya subjected their newborn children, and also at the results. Yet according to the Maya mindset, molding their babies' skulls in this way, at a time when they were still soft and easily malleable, was one of the most valuable gifts that they could give their offspring. For by trying to recreate in their children the physical appearance of the Maize God, whose head was imagined as being as tapering and elongated as a corncob, they hoped to ensure that their lives would be blessed, and maybe also that, like the Maize God, they would be reborn after their deaths.

Their appearance was one of the few things that Maya men and women could change in their lives. Their social hierarchy was fixed and hereditary, rather than fluid and free, with kings and royalty occupying the top spots and those from noble families comprising the élite, who, as priests, scribes, traders, military commanders, and administrators,

occupied the most influential positions within Maya society. And beneath them were the ordinary people, who might inherit, or rise to, modest positions of authority within their particular fields of work, but who were otherwise limited to making a living and feeding their families through farming, hunting, and fishing, through undertaking such crafts as weaving, through bartering, and through warriorship.

The Maya did not believe that death was the end for them when their time on earth was over. For they expected to embark on a journey into the afterlife that would first take them to the underworld, the dreaded *xibalba*, or "place of fright," where rivers of pus and blood flowed. Here, they believed, death gods and demonic beings would torment and try to destroy them, as they had Hun Hunahpu and his brother Vucub Hunahpu, according to the *Popol Vuh*, the sacred book of the Quiché Maya. But if they survived the horrors of *xibalba*, they fervently hoped to emulate the Hero Twins and their father, the Maize God, in emerging from the underworld and then rising to the celestial realm, where they would remain for eternity.

Mayanists have cause to be grateful for this conception of life after death, for it meant that the Maya went to their graves equipped with items that they thought they would need in the after-life, be it for survival or to smooth their passage. And the painted ceramic vessels, jade masks (see, for instance, pages 188 to 189), incensarios and funerary urns (see pages 190 to 197, for example), and other artifacts that archeologists have recovered from ancient Maya graves have proved invaluable sources of information about the lives, times, ideas, and beliefs of their long-deceased makers and owners.

Royalty and Rituals

As the hereditary rulers of Maya city-states, it may well be that Maya kings were considered to be divine, or semidivine, but even if they were regarded merely to be human, they must have been treated like gods on earth by their subjects. Yet while there is no doubt that they were immensely privileged in comparison to ordinary men and women, the lives of Maya rulers were by no means undemanding. For if not the deities' representative on earth, the king was certainly believed to be the first point of contact with the divine realm, meeting the needs of deified ancestors and other gods being his primary responsibility. If he failed, it was thought that the gods would punish him and his subjects through the infliction of such natural disasters as a drought that would cause the maize crop to fail, causing famine, suffering, and death.

Opposite, top: The ultimate purpose of most of the plazas, pyramidal temples, and other structures built by the Maya within their ceremonial city centers was to enable ritual communion with the deities.

Opposite, bottom: A detail from Lintel 25 at Yaxchilán portrays Lady Xok gazing up at the deified ancestor who is emerging from the mouth of a Vision Serpent that she has conjured up with an autosacrificial ritual. For more details, see pages 119 to 121.

Below: Many of the buildings at the now ruined site of Yaxchilán were constructed on terraced platforms. Among them are Structure, or Temple, 23, which contained the famous trio of carved lintels known as Lintel 24, Lintel 25, and Lintel 26.

Upholding the cosmic order by sustaining and honoring the gods was therefore a ruler's main duty, this being symbolized by the ceremonial bar, or double-headed serpent bar, that kings are often depicted holding in both hands (for an example, see pages 78 to 79). Scepters feature greatly in portrayals of kings, too, notably the Manikin Scepter, a miniature representation of K'awil (or God K)—see pages 146 to 148—a deity especially associated with the concept of legitimate rulership. Less distinctive examples also convey the idea of inherited divine authority, as seen, for instance, in Copán's Altar Q, where a scepter is shown being passed like a baton between the dynasty's first and last kings (see pages 132 to 135). Other aspects of the iconography of divinely sanctioned kingship include the interwoven motif representing the mat on which an important man might sit (see pages 78 to 79)—indeed, the Maya sometimes referred to their ruler as *ah pop*, "he of the mat")—and a headband displaying an image of the Jester God (see pages 142 to 145). In addition, the stone stelae and other monuments that were erected in the ceremonial centers of Maya cities portray the rulers dressed in elaborate costumes that identify them with important gods (including the Maize God), with headdresses being especially significant elements of such royal ritual regalia.

Many Maya stelae were set in place to commemorate the Long Count period-ending rites that numbered among the many rituals that rulers were required to perform on important dates or to mark dynastically significant occasions. Other members of royal families were also expected to play their parts: as pictured in Yaxchilán's lintels 24 and 25 (see pages 119 to 121), for example, rulers' wives performed acts of autosacrifice—bloodletting, in this case from the tongue—in order to conjure up deified ancestors via a Vision Serpent. Kings, too, offered their blood to the gods, typically piercing their penises until the blood flowed on to prepared strips of paper that were then burned, the smoke produced being envisaged as carrying the essence of the royal blood up to the celestial regions.

Warfare and Sacrifice, Tribute and Trade

The deities demanded blood to sustain and placate them, the Maya believed, and there were crucial ritual occasions—such as the dedication of a new temple or ballcourt, see pages 47 to 49—when not even royal blood given by means of a painful autosacrificial ritual would suffice. It was then that a ruler often dressed for war, typically in a helmet

and padded tunic, or in a jaguar skin (see pages 142 to 145 and 168 to 173), and set out with his warriors for a nearby settlement with the aim of taking captives to sacrifice to the gods, a fellow king being the ultimate prize. (This fate befell Copán's King Eighteen Rabbit, see pages 80 to 81). A mural at Bonampak shows in graphic detail the aftermath of such a military expedition, with the king, surrounded by his warriors and courtiers, standing above an abject array of captives, one of whom has already been beheaded (see pages 164 to 167).

The climax of many publicly staged ancient Maya rituals was therefore the sacrificial killing of cap-

tives, usually by decapitation—but also through the extraction of their hearts, or heart sacrifice—after which their severed heads might be displayed on skull racks, a *tzompantli* being a permanent fixture at Chichén Itzá, for example (see pages 24 to 26). Not all captives were destined for death, however, with some instead being enslaved.

Not only did martial victories supply sacrificial victims and bestow status-enhancing glory on the victorious rulers and their cities, but they also helped to decide the balance of power in a region. This had economic advantages for the most powerful city-states, in the form of the tribute that they demanded be paid to them by their weaker neighbors. The scene painted on the ceramic vessel shown on pages 174 to 179 provides a picture of the sorts of items that were given in tribute—cotton cloth, for instance, in which there was also a brisk trade across the Mesoamerican region.

Writing in *Relación de las Cosas de Yucatán (An Account of the Things of Yucatán/Yucatán Before and After the Conquest)*, de Landa described the importance of trade to the Maya:

Their favorite occupation was trading, whereby they brought in salt; also cloths and slaves from Tabasco and Ulúa. In their bartering they used cacao and stone counters which they had for money, and with which they bought slaves and other fine and beautiful stones, such as the chiefs wore as jewels on festal occasions. They had also certain red shells for use as money and jewels for wearing; these they carried in network purses. In their markets they dealt in all the products of the country; they gave credit, borrowed and paid promptly and without usuary.

Left: *A detail of the Oval Palace Tablet, from Palenque, shows the enthroned King Pacal being presented with a war helmet by his mother, Lady Zac-Kuk.*

Opposite: *A stucco-covered lintel from Bonampak depicts a warrior towering over his defeated foe. Rather than killing enemy soldiers in the heat of battle, the Maya aimed to take them prisoner prior to ritually sacrificing them in public ceremonies.*

Below: *The lines of skulls carved in bas-relief on the stone skull rack, or* tzompantli, *at Chichén Itzá illustrate the Maya practice of publicly displaying the skulls of decapitated sacrificial victims.*

Notable in de Landa's account are his mentions of cacao, whose beans were used a currency, as well as being ground to form the basis of a popular drink (see pages 186 to 187), and of the stones and shells that were worn as jewelry, which would have included jade, serpentine, turquoise, and obsidian, as well as *Spondylus* (spiny-oyster) and *Olividae* (olive) shells.

Maya Occupations

Regarded as a valuable commodity across Mesoamerica, cloth was woven by Maya women on backstrap looms, from thread spun from fibers of the cotton plant (*Gossypium hirsutum*). Elaborate designs were sometimes woven into, or embroidered on to, the cloth, which was used, among other things, as the basis of Maya clothing. (Typical ancient Maya clothing included loincloths for the men, and skirts and blouses for the women, sometimes topped with capes and cloaks). Numbering among the artisans of Maya society were also those who specialized in producing adornments from feathers; basketmakers; and the potters who created sophisticated ceramic vessels, incensarios (incense-burners), and earthenware figures, such as the lifelike examples discovered at Jaina Island (see, for instance, pages 184 to 185).

As de Landa observed, however, "The commonest occupation was agriculture, the raising of maize and the other seeds; these they kept in well-constructed places and in granaries for sale in due time." While maize was the staple food of the Maya, and therefore their most important crop, others included beans and squashes. Certain creatures were domesticated and kept for food, too, such as turkeys, and possibly dogs and deer. Maya men also hunted animals and birds with blowguns (see pages 113 to 115) and fished with nets and other implements.

Situated far higher up the social scale from manual and skilled workers and ordinary farmers, fishermen, and soldiers were the Maya traders, city and regional administrators and governors, and high-ranking warriors. The scribes whose glyphs and images have taught Mayanists so much about the Maya culture came from the upper levels of Maya society, too (see pages 174 to 179).

Those who entered the Maya priesthood were typically also from noble families, and did so, it seems, largely because this was their family "business" (see also pages 184 to 185). De Landa writes of there being different types of priests, such as the *nacóne*, who performed heart sacrifices on human victims and "was chosen as a general for the wars";

Above: *The House of the Doves (or Pigeons) at Uxmal is so named because its roof combs look rather like the dovecotes seen in Europe. In fact, it may have been a palace.*

Opposite: *Maya priests officiated at the sacred ceremonies held in the sanctuaries, or temples, at the top of pyramids like the Pyramid of the Magician at Uxmal, pictured here.*

Right: *This circular building, called the Caracol, at Chichén Itzá is believed to have served as an observatory, the astronomers who gazed at the night sky from it most likely having been Maya priests (see also page 31).*

the *chiláne*, who proclaimed the oracles supposedly given to him by the gods, probably during shamanic trances induced by hallucinogens, incense,
dance, and music (see pages 180 to 183); as well as
diviners and healers, and *chacs*, or priestly assist-
ants. According to de Landa, the Maya also:

> *... had a High Priest whom they called Ahkin*
> *May, or also Ahaucan May, meaning Priest*
> *May, or the High Priest May. ... In him lay*
> *the key to their sciences, to which they most*
> *devoted themselves, giving counsel to the chiefs*
> *and answering their inquiries. With the matter*
> *of sacrifices he rarely took part, except on*
> *great festivals or business of much moment. He*
> *and his disciples appointed the priests for the*
> *towns, examining them in their sciences and*
> *ceremonies; put in their charge the affairs of*
> *their office, and the setting of a good example*
> *to the people; he provided their books and*
> *sent them forth. They in turn attended to the*
> *service of the temples, teaching their sciences*
> *and writing books upon them. ... They taught*
> *the sons of the other priests, and the second*
> *sons of the chiefs, who were brought to them*
> *very young for this purpose, if they found*
> *them inclined toward this office.*

As well as stargazing, consulting the almanacs contained in the codices, and ensuring that the appropriate rites corresponding to particular festivals were
performed on the correct days (see page 36), priests
presided over ceremonies focused on individual
Maya. Thus, for instance, they cast newborn babies'
horoscopes and officiated at their naming ceremonies (again, see page 36).

Death and the Afterlife

As de Landa explains, the Maya believed that "after death there was another life better than this, which the soul enjoyed after leaving the body," continuing: "The delights they said they would come into if they had been of good conduct, were by entering a place where nothing would give pain, where there would be an abundance of food and delicious drinks, and a refreshing and shady tree they called Yaxché, the Ceiba tree [i.e., the World Tree, see pages 42 to 46], beneath whose branches they might rest and be in peace forever." Envisaged as lying somewhere in the heavens, it seems that this idyllic place, where the good would enjoy a blissful afterlife for eternity, would only be reached after the deceased person's spirit had first descended to the underworld, however. Here, in the dreaded *xibalba*, the Maya expected to suffer at the hands of the death lords and their demonic allies (see page 86), fearing that neither survival nor escape were guaranteed.

Believing as the Maya did that death spelled only the end of a person's life on earth, and not of his or her existence, it followed that a newly deceased person should be well equipped with useful provisions on going to the grave. As de Landa recounts:

> *At death they shrouded the body, filled the mouth with ground maize and a drink they call koyem, and with this certain stones [most likely jade] they used for money, that food might not be lacking to him in the other life. They buried them in their houses or the vicinity, throwing some of their idols into the grave; if he was a priest they threw in some of his books; if a sorcerer his divining stones and other instruments of his office. … On the death of a chief or man of position they cremated the bodies and put the ashes in large urns, and built temples over them, as is seen to have been done in the old times in the cases there have been found at Izamal. Today it is found that they put the ashes of great chiefs in hollow clay statues.*

The presence in graves of the objects listed by de Landa has been confirmed by archeologists who have excavated ancient Maya resting places, ranging from the humblest to the grandest, such as King Pacal's tomb within the Temple of Inscriptions at Palenque (see pages 42 to 46). And it is precisely these items, and others that were interred hundreds of years ago, that have helped to shed light on the previously hidden life of the ancient Maya.

Opposite: The steep-sided pyramidal temples of Tikal are among the tallest of the ancient Maya world, and are given extra height by their roof combs. It is thought that only priests, royalty, and the highest-ranking nobility were permitted to climb to the sanctuaries situated at the top of such pyramids.

Below: Despite their now ruined state, the buildings that the ancient Maya constructed have taught Mayanists much about their lost civilization, with more still waiting to be discovered.

Altar Q, Copán

Stone, Copán, Honduras

Pairings of stelae (stone pillars, see pages 78 to 81) and altars are a feature of a number of ancient Maya city-states. It is thought that when a stela was raised to commemorate a major event in a ruler's reign, an altar was positioned alongside it so that the appropriate offerings could be made on its flat top. In common with the adjacent stelae, the surfaces of Maya altars were incised with glyphs and images, whose symbolic significance is now starting to be better understood. Once thought to represent a gathering of Maya astronomers, subsequent advances in Mayanists' interpretation of glyphs means that Copán's four-sided Altar Q, for example (one side of which is shown below), is now known to portray sixteen of this eastern Maya city's kings in chronological order. And because it gives us an insight into both the iconography of Maya kingship and the line of succession of Copán's ruling dynasty, Altar Q (which was dedicated in 776) is today regarded as a hugely important historical artifact.

The side of Altar Q reproduced here shows (Kinich) Yax Kuk Mo', the dynasty's founder (who reigned from AD 426 until about 437), passing the ruler's scepter or staff—a symbol of supreme royal power—to the king who commissioned the altar's creation and carving: Yax Pasaj Chan Yoaat, or Yax Pasah, who ruled over Copán as its sixteenth king from 763 to around 820. Also portrayed around the altar's sides are the fourteen intervening sovereign lords of Copán, among them number thirteen in the line of kings: Waxaklahun Ubah K'awil, who ruled from 695 until his capture and decapitation in 738 by the king of Quiriguá (see pages 80 to 81). While every king is portrayed similarly enthroned, indicating both their equal status and their social elevation, differences are evident in their costumes and regalia, and, indeed, in what at first sight appears to be the decoration adorning their thrones, but which, in fact, presents glyphic components of their names, thus identifying each ruler.

See also **Front and Back of Stela A, Copán** (pages 78 to 81).

The depiction of Yax Kuk Mo' with round, gogglelike eyes suggests that he was a warrior dedicated to the service of Tlaloc, a Teotihuacan rain deity, worship of whom seems to have spread from Central Mexico. Indeed, it seems that the founder of Copán's royal dynasty may have been a warlord from Tikal.

The figure above, depicted in the corner of the altar next to Yax Kuk Mo', is the king who succeeded the founder of the ruling dynasty, whom Mayanists call "Ruler 2," whose reign began, it is thought, in 437.

Mayanists think that Yax Kuk Mo' is sitting on a version of the *ahau* or *ajaw* ("lord") glyph (above).

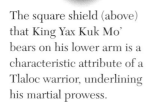

The square shield (above) that King Yax Kuk Mo' bears on his lower arm is a characteristic attribute of a Tlaloc warrior, underlining his martial prowess.

When translated Kinich Yax Kuk Mo' means Green Quetzal Macaw (Kinich is a royal title). This name's elements have been rendered within the king's headdress in pictorial, glyphic form (right).

The two glyphs carved above the royal scepter denote the Calendar Round date on which Yax Pasaj Chan Yoaat acceded to Copán's throne: 6 Caban 10 Mol, or July 2, 763. (If you look carefully at the upper glyph, you'll see that the two outer dots alongside the bar have been excised, so that the remaining central dot and bar together signify "6.")

King Yax Kuk Mo' is portrayed in the act of passing the scepter that he grasps in his hand (right) to Yax Pasaj Chan Yoaat, a symbolic action intended to underline the direct line of succession from the first to the sixteenth king, and consequently the legitimacy of Yax Pasaj Chan Yoaat's occupation of the throne of Copán.

Like those of his fellow rulers, Yax Pasaj Chan Yoaat's body is depicted facing the viewer, but with his head turned toward King Yax Kuk Mo', his dynasty's founding father.

Shown sitting next to Yax Pasaj Chan Yoaat is his immediate predecessor, K'ak' Yipyaj Chan K'awil (or King Smoke Shell), number fifteen in the line of succession, who ruled from 749 until around 761.

Relief Depicting Kan-Xul Receiving the Crown from his Father, Pacal

c.AD 720

Carved stone, Museo de Palenque, Chiapas, Mexico

The detail reproduced opposite is part of a carved stone—today known as the Palace Tablet—that was discovered in the area of Palenque's palace that archeologists call House A–D. While largely inscribed with glyphs, it also includes a figurative section showing three people seated on a trio of thrones, which, scholars speculate, may be symbolically linked to the three [hearth]stones of creation (see also pages 98 to 99). Shown on the left is King Pacal, who reigned over Palenque from AD 615 to 683 (see pages 42 to 46 and 149 to 151); in the center is his son, King Kan-Xul II (who is also known by Mayanists as K'an-Hok'-Chitam II and Kinich Kan Joy Chitam II), the ruler of Palenque from 702 to 711; and on the right (but not visible here) is Pacal's wife and Kan-Xul's mother, Lady Ahpo-Hel. Both of his parents are portrayed presenting Kan-Xul with dynastic heirlooms symbolizing royal authority and rulership. In Pacal's case, the heirloom is a headdress that we would today equate with a crown, while the martial emblem known as the tok-pakal, or "flint-shield," is held in Lady Ahpo-Hel's hands.

The obvious interpretation of this scene is that it depicts the symbolic transfer of power from a father and enthroned king to his son and legitimate heir, and consequently confirms Kan-Xul's status as Palenque's rightful ruler. Yet the historical truth is rather more complex. For, firstly, the line of succession did not initially pass directly from his father to Kan-Xul, but instead to another of Pacal's sons: to Chan-Balum II, who ruled Palenque from 684 to 702. And, secondly, Kan-Xul was long dead by the time that the Palace Tablet was completed and dedicated, having been captured and subsequently beheaded by the king of the neighboring city of Toniná in 711. Indeed, it seems that the secondary texts that can be seen in this detail do not relate to Kan-Xul at all, but may instead refer to a regent, or to his successor, or even to the headdress depicted so prominently here.

See also **Relief Showing Upacal Kinich** (pages 149 to 151).

Because both flower and creature live in water, which the Maya associated with the underworld, *xibalba*, it may be that their inclusion was intended to signal that Pacal is no longer of the earthly world.

Although he is depicted on a level with his son, Pacal is portrayed in profile, suggesting that his attention is fully focused on the significant object that he is offering Kan-Xul.

Mayanists have identified the front section of Pacal's headdress as representing a water-lily flower, to which is attached a fish, blooming above a water-lily pad.

Pacal is pictured presenting his son with a headdress or crown, an inherited symbol of the king of Palenque's right to rule. Called a war helmet, or "drum-major" headdress, by Mayanists, it features an ostentatious plume of feathers. There is also a Jester God ornament—which is frequently seen adorning the headdresses of Maya kings—fixed to the front (see also page 142).

A snarling jaguar's head (above) and a curving paw protrude from the side of Pacal's throne. Adorned as its head is with a water lily, this must be the Water Lily Jaguar, a deity that has underworld associations, and that, like all jaguars, may also be a symbol of royalty and rulership (see also pages 142 to 145).

Although he is shown gazing sideways (right) at the headdress that his father is presenting to him, his frontal position (and, in the entire image, also his central position), with his body facing the viewer, emphasizes King Kan-Xul's importance as the living inheritor of his deceased father's crown.

The top three glyphs in this inscription (left) spell out the date 1 Ahau 3 Uayeb, followed by the statement "he was born."

Another jaguar is represented at the center of the pectoral (chest) ornament that Kan-Xul is wearing.

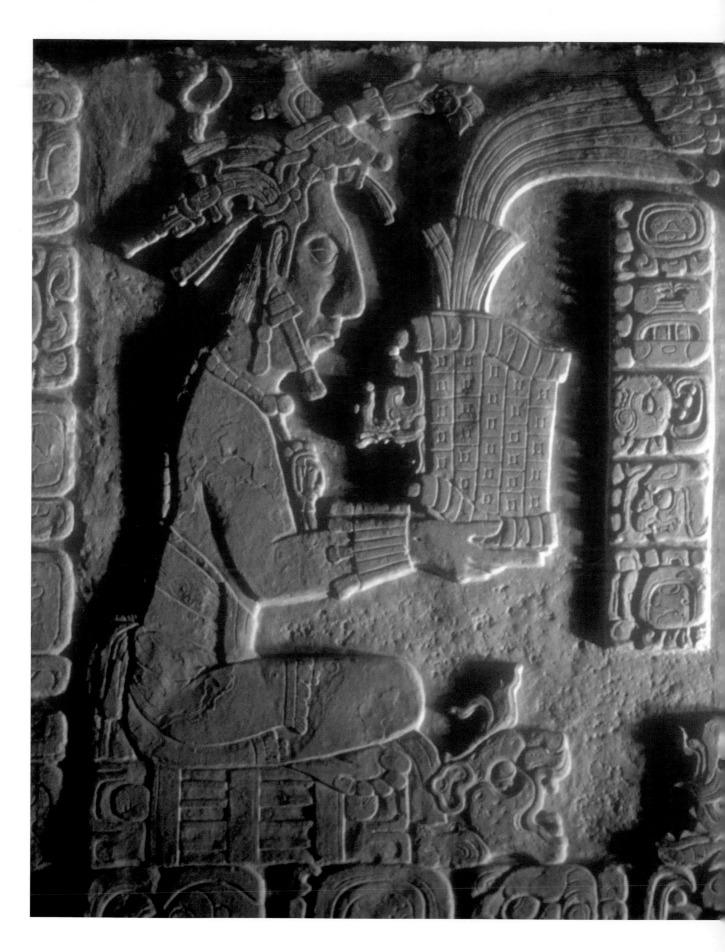

Scholars have suggested that the back of Kan-Xul's throne represents the Oval Palace Tablet (c.AD 652), which, although it is not discernible here, presents a similar scene to that illustrated in the Palace Tablet (it shows Pacal receiving the "drum-major" headdress from his mother, Lady Zac-Kuk). The inclusion in the Palace Tablet of the outline of this symbolic dynastic monument was no doubt intended to emphasize Kan Xul's rightful claim, as the son of King Pacal, to Palenque's throne.

This part (above) of the glyphic inscription states "he took office."

The creature that seems to emerge from both sides of Kan-Xul's throne is believed to be a "Xoc monster," a sharklike or saurian being (see also page 192).

Stela 35, Yaxchilán

C.AD 752–68

Stone, Yaxchilán, Chiapas, Mexico

Although it is a stela rather than a lintel, and they portray different individuals, a number of the engraved details of Yaxchilán's Stela 35, which is reproduced opposite, correspond to those depicted in Lintel 25 (see pages 119 to 121). Lintel 25 shows Lady Xok, the principal wife of Itzaam Balam II, or Shield Jaguar II, who ruled Yaxchilán between AD 681 and 742, with a Vision Serpent that she has conjured up through a bloodletting ritual, a woman and Vision Serpent also being the subject of this side of Stela 35. In this case, the woman is Lady Uh Joloom Chanil, whom Mayanists call either Lady *Ik'*-Skull or Lady Eveningstar, who is depicted on the reverse of this stela performing an autosacrificial act on a specified date that equates to 741.

Little is known about Lady *Ik'*-Skull/Eveningstar, except that she was the mother of Bird Jaguar IV, king of Yaxchilán from 752 to 768, who assumed the throne a full decade after his father, Shield Jaguar II. That ten-year gap has puzzled Mayanists, leading to speculation that there may have been a power struggle, or that Bird Jaguar may have destroyed all evidence of any other king who may have succeeded his father in an attempt to rewrite history in his favor. This stela may provide a tantalizing clue, for it was raised by Bird Jaguar to honor his mother, Lady *Ik'*-Skull/Eveningstar, who was probably a princess from Calakmul whom his father took as a lesser, or junior, wife to Lady Xok. Shield Jaguar had, it is thought, three consorts, making it likely that he had at least two sons, and it may consequently be that they disputed the line of succession after their father's death (indeed, it is believed that King Yopaat Balam II assumed the throne for part of the decade-long "inter-regnum"). Whatever happened, it is notable that Bird Jaguar erected monuments—see also pages 146 to 148—featuring his mother (who, unlike Lady Xok, received no such tribute from her husband), suggesting that he may have done so in order to promote her importance and thus justify and proclaim his own legitimacy as his father's rightful heir and king of Yaxchilán. This hypothesis is partly supported by Stela 35's subject matter—the dutiful undertaking of a painful autosacrificial ritual by a royal woman of the highest rank—and similarity to Lintel 25, which seem to place Lady Xok and Lady *Ik'*-Skull/Eveningstar on an equally prestigious footing. It is also partly supported by the glyphic inscription, which states that the woman portrayed is Bird Jaguar's mother, depicted a year before Shield Jaguar's death.

See also **Lintel 25, Yaxchilán** (pages 119 to 121) and **Lintel 53, Yaxchilán** (pages 146 to 148).

Incorporated into Lady *Ik'*-Skull's large headdress is a skull at the forefront (which some Mayanists have identified as a monkey skull). Above that, and beneath a plume of feathers, curves a detail that they identify as a skeletal serpent.

These three orbs (above) are thought to represent eyeballs, symbols of death.

Scholars have suggested that this monstrous-looking head (below) may be that of a Vision Serpent.

On her right palm, Lady *Ik'*-Skull appears to be balancing a smaller version of the monkey skull and skeletal serpent that can be seen in her headdress.

Apparently including a distended serpent's jaw, this detail may show the other end of the double-headed Vision Serpent conjured up by Lady *Ik'*-Skull. (Compare it with, for example, the lower of the Vision Serpent's heads seen on page 121.)

Decorative medallions featuring faces adorn Lady *Ik'*-Skull's broad collar, whose design matches her cuffs. Such plaques may have been fashioned from costly jade in real life.

These two glyphs (above) give a Calendar Round date: 4 Imix 4 Mol (with the 4s being signified by the four dots to the left of each glyph).

Although they are rather unclear, the fingers that can be discerned as part of this glyph suggest that it may be the "fish-in-hand" glyph, as Mayanists refer to it, or *tsak*, which means "to conjure," referring to the conjuring-up of a Vision Serpent through bloodletting.

The lady grasps a bowl containing bloodletting paraphernalia (above, including what looks like a rope and strips of paper) in her left hand, indicating that she has just performed an act of autosacrifice. (For a similar detail, see page 121.)

This glyph gives the name that Mayanists have interpreted as "Lady *Ik'*-Skull."

Lintel 26, Yaxchilán

Limestone, Museo Nacional de Antropologia, Mexico City, Mexico

The scene shown opposite is the upper portion of Lintel 26, the third of a trio of lintels that was discovered above three doorways in the building known as Structure 23, or Temple 23, in Yaxchilán. Two of these lintels portray Yaxchilán's one-time king, Itzaam (or Itzammaaj) Balam II—otherwise known as Shield Jaguar II—who reigned from AD 681 to 742, and three, Lady Xok, the woman whom scholars have identified as his principal wife. While Lintel 24 (the first in the series) portrays Lady Xok performing an act of autosacrifice by drawing blood from her tongue, Lintel 25 (the second) represents her gazing up at the Vision Serpent that she has conjured up through her bloodletting (see pages 119 to 121). And Lintel 26, which has sustained some damage, depicts Shield Jaguar dressed for battle in a warrior's quilted tunic as Lady Xok presents him with his war helmet or headdress, which takes the form of a jaguar's head (for more on the significance of this creature's symbolism in relation to war and royalty, see pages 152 to 153). Note that neither the knife that Shield Jaguar holds in his right hand nor the shield that his wife is giving him in addition to his helmet are visible in this detail.

Mayanists believe that this sculpted limestone image commemorates Shield Jaguar's ritualized preparations for leading a military attack on a neighboring Maya settlement in order to procure captives to sacrifice to the gods (see also pages 161 to 173). It is not certain exactly when this took place, but the glyphic inscriptions on the lintel provide calendrical details that equate to dates in February 724 and June 726. Structure 23 was dedicated in 726, it is thought, so it may be that sacrificial victims were required as a crucial part of the ceremonies connected with this event, and that Shield Jaguar is portrayed being equipped with the martial accouterments that would help to secure their capture.

See also **Lintel 25, Yaxchilán** (pages 119 to 121) and **Maya Lord in Cacaxtla** (pages 152 to 153).

Seen in profile, the shape of Shield Jaguar's head, with its backward-sloping brow, resembles that of a corncob. Modeled on depictions of the Maize God, the Maya considered this to be the ideal head shape. In order to achieve it, they sandwiched newborn babies' soft skulls between two wooden boards for a few days.

When viewed from the side, as here, it is evident that the ear flares, or decorations, worn by the Maya élite were extraordinarily large and ornate.

Shield Jaguar's ornate headdress culminates in a plume of quetzal feathers, a symbol of royalty. At the front, above the two floral ornaments, is the Jester God element of his headband, which is often shown decorating kings' headdresses.

Shield Jaguar wears a warrior's padded and quilted cotton tunic (detail above) to protect him from injury in battle.

Its lolling tongue gives the impression that Lady Xok is holding the decapitated head of an actual jaguar. The feathers behind it indicate that this is a headdress or helmet, however, while the floral element on top of its head suggests that it represents a jaguar deity that Mayanists call the Water Lily Jaguar.

Known as the "toothache glyph" (because it looks like the head of someone with toothache bandaged in the traditional way, with the knot tied on top of the head), the glyph above refers to a ruler's accession.

The faint, curling lines that have been traced on Lady Xok's cheeks are thought to represent the blood that still stains her skin following a bloodletting ritual of the type depicted in Lintel 24, in which she is shown threading a thorn-studded cord through her tongue.

Some scholars believe that the motif that appears to have been woven into, or embroidered on to, the fabric of Lady Xok's gown (detail above) represents a frog.

Lintel 53, Yaxchilán

c.AD 752–68

Limestone, Museo Nacional de Antropologia, Mexico City, Mexico

The clarity of the carving of Yaxchilán's Lintel 53, shown opposite, may have faded with age, but the sheer bulk of the ceremonially dressed figure on the right, along with the height of his elaborate head-dress, means that there is no mistaking his importance. He is King Itzaam Balam II, or Shield Jaguar II, of Yaxchilán (whose reign began in AD 681 and ended in 742). Opposite him stands Lady Uh Joloom Chanil, originally a princess from Calakmul and the king's third wife, scholars believe, who they call Lady *Ik'*-Skull or Lady Eveningstar. Shield Jaguar and Lady *Ik'*-Skull/Eveningstar were the parents of Bird Jaguar IV, who ruled Yaxchilán from 752 to 768, and who commissioned this lintel. The decade-long gap between his father's death and Bird Jaguar's accession to Yaxchilán's throne points to a possibly disputed line of succession (for more on this, see pages 140 to 141), which Mayanists believe explains the number of monuments emphasizing his mother's status as Shield Jaguar's wife that Bird Jaguar erected once he was safely enthroned. For while Shield Jaguar honored his first wife, Lady Xok, in this way—see pages 119 to 121 and 142 to 145—it seems that he raised no monuments at all to his third, Lady *Ik'*-Skull/Eveningstar.

Every aspect of Lintel 53, in the building known as Structure 55, is therefore intended to confirm and underline Bird Jaguar's inherited right to rule Yaxchilán, from the Manikin Scepter (a royal attribute) that his dazzlingly dressed father holds in his right hand to the prominent inclusion of his regally dressed mother holding a sacred or accession bundle, a significant ancestral symbol that often featured in dynastic rituals. (Indeed, in the *Popol Vuh*, the sacred book of the Quiché Maya, it is told that on the death of Balam Quitze, the first man to be created, he left behind a bundle called Bundled Glory, which his descendants subsequently venerated as a memorial to their earliest ancestor.) Although they seem static, the royal couple are, in fact, performing a ritual dance while displaying these symbols of sacred and royal authority. And although it was created during Bird Jaguar's reign, the lintel's glyphic inscription has been backdated, so that it states that this ritual took place in 709.

See also **Lintel 25, Yaxchilán** (pages 119 to 121).

Although it is not certain exactly what it encloses, the large bundle that Lady *Ik'*-Skull/Eveningstar is holding would have been regarded as a precious ancestral object and dynastic heirloom. In the *Popol Vuh*, the bundle left to his descendants by Balam Quitze, the first human, is described as follows: "Bundled Glory, it was called. Its contents were not clear for it was truly bundled. They did not unwrap it, nor was its stitching clear. No one had seen it when it was bundled."

It is known, however, that some sacred bundles contained the bones of ancestors or important individuals, and that the equipment required for autosacrificial rituals was wrapped within others.

A large ceremonial bar—a symbol of the sky and the Milky Way, and also of the king as the divinely approved upholder of the cosmic order—is displayed across Shield Jaguar's chest (detail below). (For another ceremonial bar, or stylized double-headed serpent bar, see pages 78 to 79.)

Shield Jaguar's ceremonial "wings" (right) were probably created by attaching quetzal feathers (royal symbols) to a supportive backrack.

His diminutive stature and serpent's foot identify the miniature figure above as K'awil (God K, according to the Schellas system of names, or GII of the Palenque Triad, see also pages 106 to 108), who, in Shield Jaguar's right hand, takes the form of the Manikin Scepter, a symbol of royal descent, divine sanction, and legitimate kingship.

Medallions featuring stylized faces adorn the king's torso. The costume that he wears is associated with period-ending rituals.

This section of the glyphic inscription to the right of the royal woman may identify her as Lady *Ik'*-Skull.

Relief Showing Upacal Kinich

c.AD 722–36

Polychrome stucco panel, Museo de Palenque, Chiapas, Mexico

Pictured at right is a section of an exquisitely detailed stucco panel that was discovered in Palenque in 1998, in the ruined structure known as Temple XIX. Although it has been damaged, when viewed in its entirety, it presents a full-length portrait of the striding Maya male who is seen in profile here, from the top of his enormous headdress right down to his toes. A now separate segment of the panel presents a number of glyphs that have helped Mayanists to conclude that this athletic-looking figure is likely to represent Upacal Kinich (or Upakal K'inich), who, as King Upacal Kinich Janaab Pacal II, ruled Palenque from around AD 736 to 742 as the successor to Kinich Ahkal Mo' Nahb III (the two may have been brothers, or else father and son). And while this stucco panel was originally situated on the eastern side of the central pier inside Temple XIX, a stone panel positioned at the front of the pier depicts a similarly portrayed—albeit far larger—Kinich Ahkal Mo' Nahb.

Despite having identified the striding individual as Upacal Kinich, depicted, it is thought, while still heir to Kinich Ahkal Mo' Nahb, there is still much about this image that remains mysterious. Scholars continue to puzzle over the iconography of Upacal Kinich's headdress, for example, which represents an enormous bird's bill with a fish dangling from its upper tip (this is not visible here), suggesting that Upacal Kinich is pictured apparently emerging from a water bird's open beak. (It has been proposed that this headdress represents a cormorant rather than a heron, but it may be that this costume is symbolically connected with a heron-with-fish glyph seen elsewhere on the Palenque site.) Given that both Kinich Ahkal Mo' Nahb and Upacal Kinich are shown wearing similar costumes in their Temple XIX portrayals, it is likely that these commemorate related rites or ceremonies, and possibly preaccession rituals of a significance and nature that are as yet unknown.

See also **The Lid of King Pacal's Sarcophagus** (pages 42 to 46).

At first sight, it may look like a wing, but this section (below) of the curved component beneath Upacal Kinich's arm is actually the lower part of the water bird's beak.

A few teeth can be seen around the area of Upacal Kinich's armpit (left).

Scholars have interpreted these glyphs as including the title *ch'ok*, which indicates a young royal. And the part of the panel that has become detached from the main section reproduced here includes glyphs that would once have been positioned above these. They spell out Upacal Kinich's name, together with the title *baah ch'ok*, which signifies "head prince," denoting a ruler's designated heir, or the next in line to the throne.

The elegant gesture that Upacal Kinich is making with his hand, and his look of concentration as he does so, have both been masterfully portrayed (details below).

These frameworks were probably made of a strong, but light, material, such as wicker (below).

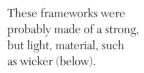

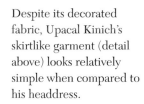

Despite its decorated fabric, Upacal Kinich's skirtlike garment (detail above) looks relatively simple when compared to his headdress.

Triangular teeth trace the outline of the bottom of the gigantic bird's upper beak, which opens just above Upacal Kinich's head.

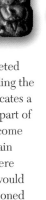

Upacal Kinich's large ear decorations, ostentatious, beaded collar, and matching wristlet signal his wealth and importance.

The elaborate headdresses and other elements of the decorative and symbolic ceremonial costumes worn for Maya rituals were supported by backracks strapped to the wearer's back.

Maya Lord in Cacaxtla

AD 650–900

Mural, Cacaxtla, Tlaxcala, Mexico

The importance of the jaguar (*Panthera onca*) to the Maya—to whom it was a symbol of ferocity and warfare, of the night and underworld, and of royalty and shamanic powers—is breathtakingly illustrated in the colorful murals discovered at Cacaxtla, which is today situated within the Mexican state of Tlaxcala. Between AD 650 and 900, Cacaxtla was a thriving city that had been founded, it is believed, by Maya settlers from the west who subsequently absorbed certain Central Mexican cultural influences. Many murals decorate the walls of the ceremonial buildings that were constructed at this hilltop location above the Tlaxcala Valley, with those in Building B (as Mayanists now call it) depicting either actual or ritualized battles between warriors with jaguar accouterments, on the one hand, and those with avian headdresses, on the other.

The figure shown opposite is one of four painted on either side of a central doorway in Building A, this one appearing on the northern jamb. It clearly portrays a human male, yet only his face and form are recognizable as such, for he mostly has a jaguar's pelt for skin and clawed jaguar's paws for hands and feet. It is not certain who this jaguar–lord is meant to be. He may represent a Maya ruler or lord, wearing the appropriate ritual costume, performing a rain- or war-related rite (the jaguar being a symbol of royalty, strength, and bravery, jaguar elements featured in royal regalia, with Maya kings also dressing themselves in jaguar pelts before going into battle). It may alternatively be that his jaguar skin links him symbolically with his *uay* (spirit alter ego, see pages 193 to 195), or with the Jaguar God of the Underworld (see pages 116 to 118), the night-time incarnation of the sun god, Kinich Ahau. However, the inclusion of a snake and a water-filled vessel bearing his portrait or symbol in this mural has led some Mayanists to believe that the figure personifies Tlaloc, the Central Mexican equivalent of the Maya rain and lightning god Chac (see pages 102 to 105), who was often depicted with jaguar fangs and sometimes also with water lilies (*Nymphaea*) in the form known as Tlaloc A.

See also **The Rain God Chac** (pages 102 to 105).

A light-colored mask portraying the head of a snake or long-jawed saurian creature surmounts the jaguar's head, beneath which the jaguar–lord's face is visible. An ostentatious plume of long, blue feathers emphasizes his high social standing and powerful status.

The jaguar–lord's face emerges from beneath a jaguar's head (complete with white fang and large eye, detail right). He himself wears a prominent nose adornment.

The jaguar–lord grasps the long, sinuous body of a snake in the claws of his left-hand paw. The tan-colored line that marks its underside can be traced running from the serpent's head, which can be seen amid the feathers of his headdress, to its curled tail, which hangs in front of the lord's thigh.

A flower and shoot of foliage seem to sprout from its body in a possible reference to the life-giving powers of fertility associated with snakes. Serpents can represent water in Mayan art, too (a connection to which this snake's predominantly blue body may point), as well as the sky, and also, in the hands of the rain deities Tlaloc and Chac, lightning.

The jaguar–lord encourages water to spill from a vase that he clutches and cradles in the crook of his right arm. The vessel appears to have been decorated with the stylized face or symbol of Tlaloc, the goggle-eyed Central Mexican rain god.

A flowering plant seems to have sprouted from the jaguar–lord's navel. Apparently growing vigorously, it has nearly reached the water in which he is standing. That both plant and water are colored blue may underline a symbolic connection, while the flowers signify fertility. And if the flower is interpreted as a water lily, it may furthermore denote standing water and thus a living link between the earthly world and the underworld, which the Maya envisaged as being a watery realm.

Although his body is covered in jaguar fur rather than human skin, and his feet and hands are viciously clawed jaguar's paws, the jaguar–lord wears unmistakably human garments and adornments.

Relief Showing a Seated Man Wearing Magnificent Robes and a Headdress of Feathers

AD 615–83

Jade, from the Temple of Inscriptions, Palenque, Museo Nacional de Antropologia, Mexico City, Mexico

Following the discovery of King Pacal's funerary crypt within the Temple of Inscriptions in Palenque in 1952, the treasures that had been placed alongside Pacal's sarcophagus (see pages 42 to 46) were painstakingly removed and examined. Among them was the jade relief pictured opposite, whose fluidly carved, lifelike lines portray a man whose exact identity is unknown, but whose youthful, idealized features and elaborate personal adornments place him at the highest level of Maya society at the time of King Pacal's reign (AD 615–83).

Although costly clothing was worn, particularly for ritual purposes, a loincloth was the normal attire for elite Maya men, the custom instead being to use jewelry and headdresses as a visual means of displaying their importance and impressing others. When his sarcophagus was opened, the corpse of King Pacal himself was found to be bedecked in jade jewelry, testifying to the value—both real and symbolic—that the Maya accorded to jade, and providing examples of the types and styles of jewelry worn by royal and aristocratic men. A necklace, ear ornament, wristlets, and anklet can clearly be seen in this relief, and collars, pendants, and pectorals (ornaments worn on the chest), as well as jewelry designed to decorate the head, fingers, and belt, were also worn by high-class Maya males. Such pieces were typically made of jade and alternative greenstones, obsidian, mother-of-pearl and other shells, and also of bone and feathers. The most spectacular element of a king or lord's costume was, however, the headdress, which was frequently huge and colorful, usually featuring jewel-hued feathers plucked from the bodies of macaws and other tropical birds. The feathers that were the most sought-after were the long, emerald-green tail feathers of the elusive male quetzal bird (*Pharomachrus mocinno*), their rarity and beauty causing them to become a symbol of royal authority—indeed, the names of many Maya kings incorporate the word *k'uk'*, as the Maya called the quetzal.

See also **The Lid of King Pacal's Sarcophagus** (pages 42 to 46).

Long feathers have been fixed to the man's elaborate headdress. Worn by kings, quetzal feathers signified royalty and power to the Maya.

Wristlets, or bracelets, as well as anklets, were commonly worn by noble Maya men.

Seen in profile (right), the long line that can be traced from the tip of the man's nose to the top of his forehead conforms to the ideal set by images of the Maya Maize God (see pages 62 and 96), whose representation was in turn based on the tapering, elongated appearance of a ripe corncob.

There is evidence that wellborn Maya achieved this effect both by flattening newborn babies' soft skulls between two boards for a few days, and, in adulthood, by building up the bridges of their noses by artificial means.

Jewelry apart, the man is dressed according to Maya convention, that is, in a decorated loincloth, with his arms, legs, and torso remaining bare.

His oversized necklace and earring signal the man's high status and wealth; in life, it is likely that these large beads would have been formed from jade.

Being extremely hard and unyielding, the jade base from which this relief was fashioned would have been difficult to work with.

This consideration, combined with the obvious expertise and artistry of its maker, tells us that it would have been regarded as a valuable artifact at the time of its creation.

In addition, jade was greatly valued by the Maya, who equated its green color with that of water and growing vegetation (especially maize), and therefore with fertility, life, and renewal.

Statuette of a Warrior

AD 650–1000

Terra cotta, Museo Nacional de Antropologia, Mexico City, Mexico

So many terra-cotta figures of warriors have been discovered within the thousands of graves that archeologists have excavated on the island of Jaina, which lies off the Campeche coast of the Yucatán Peninsula, that Mayanists speculate that at least part of this "cemetery isle" was dedicated to the burial of warlords. And perhaps not only noble warriors were interred here, but also less high-born soldiers who had distinguished themselves in battle, or who had been killed in action. In the latter case, the Maya believed that they had earned the right to be spared the posthumous trials of *xibalba* (the "place of fright," or underworld), which most others were obliged to survive before ascending to the celestial realm.

Although it has been damaged—the right hand has been destroyed, and with it probably a weapon— the warrior figure from Jaina shown opposite has nevertheless been so finely crafted that it provides a detailed picture of how Maya men dressed, and of the type of shield they carried, when preparing to engage in warfare during the Classic Period. Because certain elements of the figure's costume, such as his "wings," appear more decorative than practical, however, it is likely that the man portrayed is dressed in ceremonial military garb, and that he is of noble birth. Kings and nobles (in whom warriorship, aggression, and bravery were regarded as a prestige-enhancing virtues) automatically assumed leadership roles in martial situations, the rank and file whom they commanded being drawn from the lower levels of Maya society. And it is thought that their primary aim in launching military ventures against rival city-states was to seize captives to sacrifice to the deities on significant dynastic occasions, and the nobler, the better. This, it seems, was the fate of King Eighteen Rabbit (Waxaklahun Ubah K'awil) of Copán, who was ritually decapitated by King Cauac Sky of Quiriguá in AD 738 (see pages 80 to 81).

See also **Costumed Figure** (pages 184 to 185).

Although the man represented by this figure is dressed as a warrior, his expression is serene, rather than bellicose, perhaps in accordance with the ideal Maya appearance, which was based on representations of the Maize God (see page 62).

His high, backward-sloping forehead (a corncoblike shape achieved by sandwiching newborn babies' skulls between two boards), abundant head of cornrow-styled hair, full lips, and strong nose may similarly have been modeled on portraits of the Maize God. All of these features (which may together have presented a faithful portrait of the man with whom this figure was buried) suggest that he was a member of the Maya social élite.

An ostentatious collar, possibly constructed of feathers, covers the warrior's shoulders. The string of large beads seen beneath it falls to his navel, culminating in a huge pendant. These decorative accessories, like his wristband and visible ear decoration, are signs of high status within Maya society.

Because the wings that appear to sprout from the warrior's back would have been more of a hindrance than a help in action, it is likely that their purpose was purely ceremonial, maybe also embodying a symbolic reference to a powerful bird of prey in an attempt to channel its fighting spirit.

The originals on which the wings were based may well have been made of feathers.

The warrior holds his large, rectangular shield in his left hand. Decorated with tassels, it is strikingly similar to the shield carried by another figure from Jaina (see pages 184 to 185).

The man's right hand has been broken off, but would no doubt originally have gripped a weapon, such as a spear or a club.

The ankle-length robe that the warrior is wearing appears to have a scaly or chainmail-like texture, which may have been achieved by quilting layers of cotton in order to provide some protection against the blows of sharp weapons in battle. His garment may alternatively have been covered with feathers, or else been both quilted and feathered.

Urn Lid with a Figure of a Warrior from Guatemala AD 600–950

Terra cotta, Didrichsen Art Museum, Helsinki, Finland

The terra-cotta urn lid pictured here portrays a fierce-looking warrior, who, despite being seated (a posture that no doubt suited the lid's design requirements better than a standing position), appears to be on the verge of attacking an approaching foe. Clutching his shield in front of him with his left hand, this passive, defensive gesture is counterbalanced by the active, offensive motion that he makes with his raised right hand, which grips a weapon.

Although they were certainly capable of inflicting lethal injuries on the enemy, most weapons were used to disarm and disable rather than to kill outright because the Maya embarked on warfare with the main aim of obtaining captives for subsequent ritual sacrifice. And because iron did not feature in Mesoamerican weaponry until its introduction following the Spanish Conquest, any cutting edge—maybe set into the top of a wooden-handled spear to provide a sharp tip, or around the head of a club—was fashioned from flint or obsidian. The *Popol Vuh*, the Quiché Maya's creation account, which was set down during the sixteenth century, describes axes being carried by warriors, along with arrows—by which may be meant short stabbing spears, see page 65 for example—and shields, which could be rectangular, as illustrated here, or rounded (see, for example, pages 168 to 173).

While his shield, which would probably have been made of wood, was the Maya warrior's main form of defense, a padded or quilted cotton tunic or vest could be worn to provide some protection against the enemy's weapons (see also page 157). In addition, a protective headdress or helmet, as seen in the depiction of the Maya warrior shown here, was intended to ward off the worst of an opponent's blows. Such martial headwear was frequently adorned with images of a patron deity or symbolic elements representing a ferocious creature, notably the jaguar and birds of prey like the eagle, in the hope that their strength and power would transferred to the warrior.

See also **Vessel with a Procession of Warriors** (pages 168 to 173).

A disembodied head is set at the forefront of the warrior's helmet. The large ear decoration and eye that are visible, along with the apparently toothless mouth, suggest that it represents a deity, such as God L, the Maya merchant god who was also linked with war during the Classic Period (see also pages 67 to 69).

The warrior's helmet and tunic are adorned with a triangular motif made up of a trio of circles. This may be a purely decorative addition, but it may also be significant that the three hearth stones of the Maya creation myth are represented similarly (in the Madrid Codex, for example).

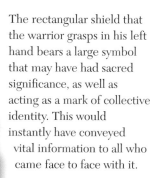

Equated with Alnitak, Saiph, and Rigel—three stars within the constellation of Orion—these three stones were said to have been set in place in the sky on the day of creation to form the first Maya cooking hearth (see also pages 95 to 97).

The warrior is wearing a protective tunic (right) that covers his shoulders, as well as his torso.

The weapon that the warrior brandishes in his right hand appears to be either a club—possibly flint-edged—or a hafted ax. (It could be a head-shaped stone ax, or *hacha*, although most surviving examples seem to have been used in ballgame-related rituals rather than on the battlefield).

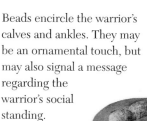

Beads encircle the warrior's calves and ankles. They may be an ornamental touch, but may also signal a message regarding the warrior's social standing.

The rectangular shield that the warrior grasps in his left hand bears a large symbol that may have had sacred significance, as well as acting as a mark of collective identity. This would instantly have conveyed vital information to all who came face to face with it.

Battle Scene

c.800

Mural painting, Room 2 of the Painted Temple at Bonampak,
Museo Nacional de Antropologia, Mexico City, Mexico

Following their discovery in 1946, the astonishingly vivid murals that adorn the interior of a building known variously as Structure 1, Temple 1, the Temple of the Paintings, or the Painted Temple have since made the ancient Maya site of Bonampak famous. "Bonampak" means "Painted Walls," and the site lies around 19 miles (30 km) south of Yaxchilán. Considered among the finest examples of Maya artistry, these murals are notable partly for their naturalistic figurative style and partly on account of the pictorial information that they convey, from which Mayanists have learned much about various aspects of the Maya world: the costumes worn by the social élite on ceremonial occasions and in battle, for example.

The colorful murals are painted on the interior walls of three rooms within Structure 1. While the images in Room 1 relate to the rituals that marked the designation of King Chan Muan of Bonampak's heir and the subsequent dedication of the building in 790 and 791 respectively (see pages 180 to 183), those in Room 3 commemorate the celebrations and sacrificial rituals that followed the king's victory in the battle that is the subject of Room 2. Shown here is a section of Room 2's battle scene, which was painted on the east wall and illustrates battle being engaged to the sound of war trumpets. Bonampak warriors wearing splendid headdresses are already taking captives, who, in the concluding scene in Room 2's north wall, present a miserable picture of total collective defeat (see pages 164 to 167). Indeed, in accordance with Maya practice, it seems that the primary objective of this battle was to secure as many high-class prisoners as possible to sacrifice to the gods so that the deities would look with favor on Bonampak's king and his ventures, as well as his newly designated heir and the dynastic succession.

See also **Maya Warlords and Captives** (pages 164 to 167).

A trumpeter (above) purses his lips as he sounds his instrument, only a portion of which is visible here.

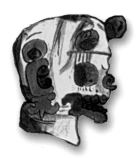

The white headdress worn by the warrior who has gained the upper hand over his enemy resembles a skull. It is an unambiguous reference to death, and maybe also to a death lord of *xibalba* (the "place of fright," or Maya underworld). The red orbs adorning it may represent eyeballs.

Pictured at the moment of his capture, a powerfully built fighter is incapacitated by the warrior behind him. He has been pinned down by the arm that stretches from his left shoulder and across his neck, with the hand gripping his torso beneath his right arm.

As well as being depicted in defeat, his inferior status as a military opponent is signaled by his lack of ear decorations and headdress, in marked contrast to his Bonampak foes.

His dark skin makes the warrior whose detail is shown below strikingly distinct from those around him. Although this skin color may have been natural, he may otherwise have painted his body black, maybe to symbolize his martial nature and purpose.

A lethal-looking spear is being pointed at the head of the combatant who has just been grabbed by a Bonampak warrior. Its spearhead would have been made from sharpened flint or obsidian, and its handle, from hard wood.

The crouching warrior at the front of this section (detail above) wears an enormous headdress that appears to have been modeled on a deer's head, or else a fabulous creature's.

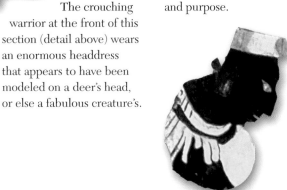

Maya Warlords and Captives c.800 (twentieth-century copy)

Watercolor, copy by Antonio de Tejeda of a mural painting in Room 2 of the Painted Temple at Bonampak, Peabody Museum, Harvard University, Cambridge, Massachusetts

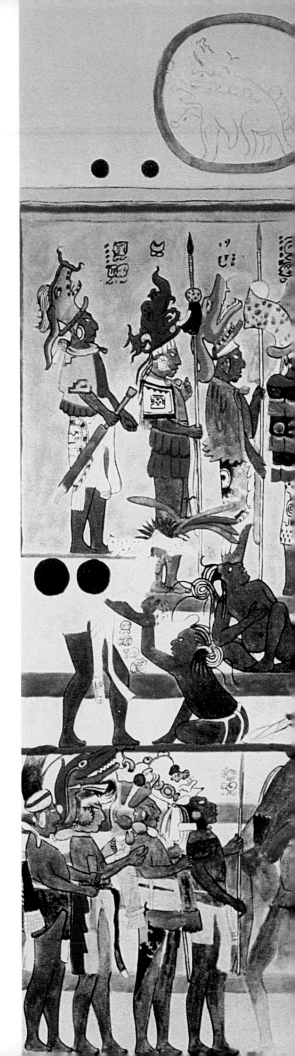

The watercolor painting shown at right is a late-twentieth-century copy of the original mural. It is, however, an exact copy, and it is a sad fact that the condition of the spectacular scenes that were painted on the interior walls of the building known as Structure 1 (or, alternatively, as Temple 1, the Painted Temple, or the Temple of the Paintings) has deteriorated since their discovery at Bonampak in 1946. This section was painted on the north wall of Room 2, whose images also illustrate a heated battle (see pages 161 to 163) that was fought, it is thought, to enable the Bonampak army to capture worthy victims to sacrifice to the gods. This was, it appears, a vital component of the rituals relating to the confirmation of King Chan Muan of Bonampak's heir and the dedication of the building, which took place in 790 and 791 respectively, and which are the subject of the murals in Room 1 (see pages 180 to 183) and Room 3.

Looking at this detailed portion of the murals, which was painted around an interior doorway, it is clear that the battle is now over and that the king of Bonampak and his army have emerged victorious. Seemingly positioned at the apex of a pyramid formed by his men and their captives, who are arranged on a series of steps, the king stands apart from the warlords, nobles, and other members of his court who flank him. His captives present a pathetic picture: trapped by their captors on the higher steps, one has already been decapitated, another is close to death—if not already dead—yet more have been brutalized, and one is actually undergoing torture. The prisoner who is sitting at the king's feet appears to be begging for mercy, but as the images in Room 3 confirm, his plea will be in vain. The captives' absolute defenselessness and humiliation is emphasized by their lack of clothing, weapons, and accouterments, for they are wearing only loincloths, in striking contrast to the elaborately attired, spear-wielding victors.

See also **Battle Scene** (pages 161 to 163).

A Bonampak captor has seized a captive (above) by the wrist. Perhaps the captor intended to torture his victim by inflicting injuries on his left hand.

A seated prisoner (above) looks fearfully upward at the array of military might ranged above his head. His hair has been pulled back and knotted in a style that seems to signify a captive in Maya art.

A disembodied head lies on a step, the grisly evidence of a decapitation that has already taken place. The gray matter in which it appears to be wreathed is most likely the brains that have spilled from the dead man's skull.

Blood is shown dripping from the hands of the prisoners seated on the left (detail below), causing Mayanists to speculate that their fingernails have been ripped out, or that their fingertips have been severed from their hands.

The jaguar skin that has been draped over his back suggests that the figure shown at right may enjoy royal status, or that he is an outstanding warrior. By wearing jaguar skins in battle, Maya warlords may also have hoped to absorb something of this predatory animal's ferociousness and fearlessness.

His sprawling, relaxed posture is in stark contrast to the tense, seated positions of his fellow captives, suggesting that this prisoner is either unconscious or already dead.

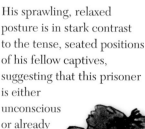

A captive (above) has been hauled in front of Chan Muan and appears to be pleading with him. The king does not even deign to look down at him, however.

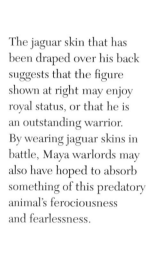

While the band running above the scene signifies the sky, the turtle on the right (detail at right) represents the constellation of Orion, and the three circles running along its back, three stars within it: Alnitak, Saiph, and Rigel. (See also pages 95 to 97 and 158 to 160.)

King Chan Muan (above) appears proud and somewhat aloof as he stands at the center of the scene, holding a spear that has been decorated with jaguar skin. The jaguar-skin elements that can also be seen in his headdress, tunic, and sandals symbolize his kingship, as well as such characteristics associated with the jaguar (which the ancient Maya regarded as the king of the beasts) as bravery, strength, and aggression. The long plumes of his headdress may represent another Maya symbol of royalty: quetzal feathers.

Her gown identifies the onlooker near the top right of the scene, holding a fan, as a woman.

She may be King Chan Muan's wife, who, it is recorded, was a member of the royal family of neighboring Yaxchilán, with which Bonampak was allied.

Bonampak soldiers (detail at right) stand to attention at the forefront of the scene, guarding the captives depicted above them.

Vessel with a Procession of Warriors

c.750–850

Earthenware, Kimbell Art Museum, Fort Worth, Texas

Scholars believe that one of the main reasons why the Maya engaged in warfare with one another was to seize prisoners. Some might be enslaved, while others would be sacrificed to the gods, in the hope that the deities would look with favor upon those who made this bloody offering. A coronation, the designation of an heir, or the dedication of a ceremonial building—as at Bonampak, for example, see pages 161 to 167—or ballcourt (see pages 47 to 49) were all events that required such ritual shedding of sacrificial blood. And the more important the sacrificial victim, the better, a king being regarded as the most prestigious prize (this fate befell King Eighteen Rabbit of Copán in 738, for instance, see pages 80 to 81). The military raids that secured the necessary victims were typically planned with reference to the Venus calendar (see Page 49 from the Dresden Codex, featured on pages 64 to 66), this planet's influence being believed to be propitious for warfare.

The image that you see on these pages is a "rollout" photograph of a scene that was painted on the outer surface of a cylindrical Maya vessel during the Late Classic Period, showing us the procession of men that appear to proceed clockwise around the vase. The shields and spears carried by four of the figures identify them as fighting men of various ranks, while the fifth man, who is depicted in their midst (see page 169), is clearly a captive who has been stripped of his clothes and weaponry and is destined for ritual decapitation. The solemn and stately impression given by the five figures, along with the victors' ceremonial clothing, suggest a ritual scenario, a calculated display of triumph and degradation performed in the aftermath of the battle in which the prisoner was captured. Indeed, he may be in the process of being led, before an audience of the victorious king's subjects, to his place of execution, maybe a sacrificial platform constructed on a temple or ballcourt.

See also **Urn Lid with a Figure of a Warrior from Guatemala** (pages 158 to 160).

The headdress of the leading warrior in the parade resembles an owl turned on its side. The "owl of omen" featured prominently in the Maya iconography of warfare, having originally been borrowed from the imagery of Teotihuacan. This bird was also associated with death and the Maya underworld, *xibalba* (see pages 50 to 55).

The sharp stick that protrudes from the front of the paper-clad man's headdress may represent a stingray spine. Serrated stingray spines were commonly used by the Maya to draw blood from the body when such offerings were required.

The pale-colored garment worn by the man preceding the captive is made from strips of bark paper, which the Maya used to soak up the blood from wounds made during autosacrificial or sacrificial rituals. The bloody paper was then burned as an offering to the gods, who were believed to receive it in the form of the smoke that drifted upward, toward the divine realm (see also pages 119 to 121). The red-dotted elements of his paper robe may have been stained with blood.

The captive's utter helplessness and humiliation is emphasized by his nakedness, and particularly by the exposure of his genitals, and also by the position of his arms, which have been twisted painfully behind his back so that he is unable to lash out. A strip of bark paper—signifying bloodletting and sacrifice—appears to have been attached to his earlobe, and the object in front of him is most likely the flint- or obsidian-bladed instrument that will be used to decapitate him.

All of the victors hold a spear and shield in their left hands. While Maya warriors carried both into battle, the combination of the spear's flint or obsidian tip (tok) and the shield (pakal) also became a martial emblem (tok-pakal, or "flint-shield").

The trefoil, or motif made up of three triangle-forming circles, that decorates this lower-ranking warrior's headdress also appears on the tunic of the man leading the procession. (Details below. For another example of the trefoil's use in relation to martial imagery, see pages 158 to 160.)

The glyphs below represent the planet Venus (*lamat*, the glyph also representing eighth day sign of the *tzolkin*, or 260-day calendar), indicating that battle was deliberately engaged on a significant date in the Venus calendar.

The magnificent jaguar skin that has been draped over this warrior's body (above) identifies him as the most powerful figure in this scene, for only military leaders wore the pelt of this predatory big cat, which symbolized royalty, as well as bravery, strength, and aggression. He may even be the king and commander-in-chief of the other warriors in the parade.

In his right hand, the commander holds aloft a bloodstained club or ax, partly, perhaps, to demonstrate his readiness to subdue his captive should he try to escape, and partly to prove to any onlookers that he himself has been in action, and has inflicted injuries on his enemies. (The Maya considered a fighting spirit and military prowess desirable qualities in a ruler.)

The decorative black patterns that can be seen on the faces of the warriors, and also on this man's upper arm and thigh, may either be permanent tattoos or may have been painted on to the skin prior to battle.

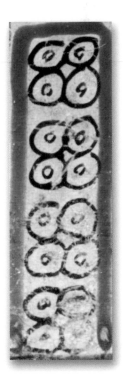

Tribute Being Paid

Date unknown

Earthenware, private collection

Pictured on these pages is a "rollout" photograph of the polychrome scene that was painted around the outside of a ceramic Maya vase, and of the accompanying glyphs that have helped Mayanists to understand what it depicts. Together, the glyphs and images have led them to conclude that what we are seeing is Lord Completion Star (Kinich Lamaw Ek') of Motul de San José (a now ruined site in Petén, Guatemala, which is equated with the "*Ik* site" specified here) conferring with two seated lord-scribes as he receives a variety of goods offered as tribute by a subordinate city-state. Effectively a tax, the payment of tribute formed a significant sector of the Maya economy. It was an important factor in the movement and distribution of such goods as cotton mantles and cacao beans (see pages 186 to 187) around the Maya region.

Scenes like this suggest that a scribe's role encompassed far more than just writing and illustrating screenfold books, or codices (see, for example, the Dresden and Madrid codices, pages 61 to 77), on all manner of subjects, or, indeed, painting ceramic vessels like the vase shown here. Mayanists believe that scribes (who underwent training at scribal schools from an early age) were drawn from the highest levels of Maya society, many being the siblings of rulers themselves. Literacy was highly prized, and the combination of their élite status and rare skills meant that scribes were important figures in Maya society, and probably played a consultative or advisory role in relation to Maya kings. In addition, as the scribal name *ah-k'uhun* ("keeper of the books") suggests, scribes acted as record-keepers—recording, for instance, details of the type of tribute paid by a city that had, perhaps, been rendered subordinate through defeat in battle—librarians, masters of ceremonies during the performance of rituals, administrators, arrangers of royal marriages, and royal genealogists. It is also possible that scribes were assigned ambassadorial roles, and that after accompanying the items making up the tribute payment to Motul de San José, those portrayed here are acting as emissaries in presenting it to Lord Completion Star on their ruler's behalf.

See also **Censer Lid with a Woman Holding Cacao** (pages 186 to 187).

The two large bundles at the feet of the man bearing goods contain some form of tribute, perhaps cotton mantles (a nearby glyph within the secondary text reads "tribute mantle").

Versatile cotton cloth was highly valued in Maya society. It was woven by women on backstrap looms from thread spun from fiber provided by the indigenous cotton plant (*Gossypium hirsutum*), often into colorful designs.

A man stands in the background (detail at left), propping up what appears to be a trumpet with his left hand and clutching a length of cloth attached to a pole—maybe a hanging, canopy, or awning—in his right hand. Both of these items form part of the tribute offered to the ruler of Motul de San José.

This (above) is the Emblem Glyph denoting the once mysterious "*Ik* site," which Mayanists have identified—first tentatively, and now with increasing confidence—with Motul de San José.

The first two glyphs directly above the main instance of secondary text (detail shown below) represent the Calendar Round date 7 Chicchan 8 Mol (note the dot-and-bar combinations to the left of these glyphs, signifying "7" and "8" respectively). They are followed by a variation on the Initial Sign of the Primary Standard Sequence (PSS) of text that was typically painted on ceramic vessels like this vase. (See also pages 55 and 59.)

The man standing behind the lord is smoking a thin cigar. The ancient Maya were well aware of the stimulant properties of tobacco (*Nicotiana*).

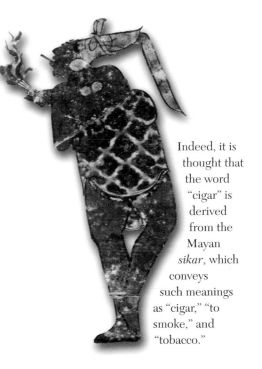

Indeed, it is thought that the word "cigar" is derived from the Mayan *sikar*, which conveys such meanings as "cigar," "to smoke," and "tobacco."

The figure to the rear of the seated men holds what seems to be a pair of flaming sticks before him (above), maybe to provide light.

Both his throne and the cloth canopy beneath which he sits highlight Lord Completion Star's elevated status. Wearing a strikingly decorated cloak, the lord of Motul de San José sits cross-legged on his throne, addressing the lord-scribes in front of him.

Stored beneath the lord's throne are a lidded cylinder vessel and a bowl containing a black obsidian mirror (mirrors were used by the Maya for divination, personal adornment, and as an aid to personal grooming). These may be tribute offerings that have already been accepted.

A Scene from Life, Depicting Musicians c.800

Mural painting, east wall of Room 1 of the Painted Temple at Bonampak, Museo Nacional de Antropologia, Mexico City, Mexico

Among the colorful and extraordinarily naturalistic murals that were painted on the interior walls of the building at Bonampak known as Structure 1 (or Temple 1, the Painted Temple or the Temple of the Paintings) are sections portraying Maya musicians and dancers. (For more Bonampak murals, see pages 161 to 167). The detail reproduced at right was painted on the east wall of Room 1, whose scenes, Mayanists believe, were dedicated to recording the rituals that were performed on the designation of a young child as the heir to Chan Muan, king of Bonampak. This dynastic event began on December 14, 790, with the formal presentation of the child to members of the nobility, followed by the dedication of the building on November 15, 791, a date that marked the planet Venus's appearance as the Evening Star (see pages 64 to 66). The detail shown here, which was painted on the lower register of the double-register mural, shows members of a procession of musicians that precedes a group of dancers.

Dance and music were vital components of the ritual occasions celebrated by the Maya, and the depictions of musicians at Bonampak and elsewhere give us not only an

idea of the types of instruments that were played (by memory or ear, since no examples of musical notation have been discovered), but also of the order in which the participants walked or danced in procession. The four musicians that we see here, for example, are beating three turtle carapaces and a large, vertical drum. They are preceded by men shaking long-handled rattles (probably seed-filled gourds) and are followed by musicians blowing huge trumpets apparently made from fired clay or wood, all of whom are out of sight here. Further instruments played by the Maya included a hand drum carried under the arm, as well as split or double drums; rasps made from bone; and whistles, flutes, ocarinas, panpipes, and conch shells fashioned from bone, wood, or fired clay. Stringed instruments were unknown at this time, however.

See also **Battle Scene** (pages 161 to 163) and **Maya Warlords and Captives** (pages 164 to 167).

Two standard bearers carry enormous long-staffed, feather-decorated battle standards. Only their legs can be seen as they walk alongside the musicians.

The inclusion of the standard bearers may be a reference to the battle recorded as following the building-dedication ceremonies, which is represented in Room 2 (see pages 161 to 163).

The musician depicted on the far right plays a drum as tall as his chest with his bare hands. This drum was probably fashioned from a hollowed-out tree trunk. The wood was decorated before the final component, a deerskin, was stretched across the top and secured in place.

All of the turtle-shell players are wearing striking headdresses.

The three musicians that are proceeding across the east wall from the left each hold drums made from turtle carapaces, which they are beating with deer antlers. The sound produced by these turtle shells resembled thunder.

The most eye-catching element of the drummer's headdress is the fish attached to a water lily at the front (detail below).

The inclusion of this aquatic creature and plant indicate that the drummer represents an inhabitant of *xibalba*, the underworld, which the Maya envisaged as being under water. Here, according to the *Popol Vuh* (the Quiché Maya's creation account), the Hero Twins danced for the death lords.

Costumed Figure 7th–8th century

Ceramic and pigment, The Metropolitan Museum of Art, New York, New York

There has been some disagreement among Mayanists as to the most likely identity of the painted ceramic figure of a man shown here, which was discovered on Jaina Island, located off the Yucatán Peninsula's Campeche coast. For while his huge headdress has, on the one hand, led some to consider him a Maya priest, his distinct potbelly and corpulent facial features have, on the other, caused others to associate him with the Fat God, a Maya deity about which relatively little is understood. Yet another school of thought regards him as a warlord—and the similarities in clothing that are evident when this figure is compared with that of a warrior illustrated on pages 156 to 157 are indeed striking.

What is certain, however, is that the figure was intended to represent a Maya man of high social status. And it is known that priests were typically drawn from the ranks of the nobility, while warriors were typically originally ordinary men whose martial occupation had raised them to the middle ranks of Maya society. It is also thought that the Maya believed that priests and warriors killed in action were among those privileged few who bypassed the horrors of *xibalba* (the "place of fright" or underworld) after their deaths, instead traveling directly to the heavenly realm. This consideration may be significant in this context, given that the figures found on Jaina, like this one—and see also pages 111 to 112 for another—were interred with the thousands of dead who were buried there. The main tasks of priests included stargazing and divination, as well as interpreting such almanacs as those contained in, for example, the Dresden and Madrid codices, overseeing sacred rites and ritual festivities, and keeping written dynastic records. But priestly and martial roles may have overlapped when it came to making offerings to the deities. For it was probably priests who sacrificed the captives taken by their city's warriors on significant ritual occasions in order to appease and sustain the gods.

See also **Statuette of a Warrior** (pages 156 to 157).

Feathers arranged as wings flank the man's extraordinarily tall headdress or helmet, which, like his large ear flares, mark him out as a person of consequence in Maya society.

The figure appears to be gripping a rectangular shield that covers the entire length of his left leg. Decorated with tassels, it closely resembles the shield held by the warrior figure shown on pages 156 to 157.

The prominent bulge (right) of his potbelly no doubt encouraged this figure's identification by some as the Fat God.

The texture of much of the figure's blue-painted costume suggests that the real-life version was densely decorated with feathers.

In addition, its rather bulky appearance suggests that it was modeled on the garments worn by Maya warriors, which included padded, or quilted, cotton in order to lend them protective qualities.

Large disks decorate the figure's feet. When interpreting the subtle messages conveyed by Maya artists and craftspeople, it seems that the more elaborate the footwear and headgear, the more important the individual depicted.

Censer Lid with a Woman Holding Cacao   AD 250–450

Earthenware, Museo Nacional de Arqueología y Etnología, Guatemala City, Guatemala

Cacao, or cocoa, the product of the cacao tree (*Theobroma cacao*), was greatly valued by the Maya, partly on account of the flavor that it yields, and partly due to its consequent worth. Indeed, as well as being traded, cacao beans were used as currency—as an organic equivalent of coins—in Mesoamerica, and also featured among tribute payments. The deity most associated with cacao was Ek Chuah (or God M), a Maya merchant god (see pages 70 to 71).

Cacao's intrinsic value to the Maya lay in the drink that was made from the beans contained within the tree's pods. Once the pods had been harvested, the beans were extracted and dried. Then, the cacao beans were ground and mixed with water, along with flavoring ingredients like chili peppers— the choice of the Maya nobility, it seems—to produce a cold drink, which, unlike the cocoa-derived chocolate that is generally preferred today, was both bitter and spicy (that is, unless it was sweetened with honey, vanilla, or other bitterness-reducing agents). Another drink made with cacao was mixed with dried maize. Such cacao-based drinks were stored in tall cylindrical vessels, from which they were poured into drinking cups from a high enough level to produce a pleasing froth. From their reading of the Primary Standard Sequence (PSS)—the glyphic text that typically appears on ceramic "vases"— Mayanists know that some vessels were specifically dedicated to the serving of cacao, for the glyph following "his [or her] vessel for drink" (*yu-k'ib*) reads *kakaw*, or "cacao," sometimes followed by further information about the exact nature of the cacao.

Many such vessels accompanied élite members of Maya society to the tomb, presumably to ensure that they would continue to enjoy their favorite cacao drink in the afterlife. Other grave finds also focus on cacao, such as the earthenware censer (incense-burner, or incensario) lid shown opposite, on which numerous cacao beans have been depicted. This object comes from Guatemala's southern coastal region, an area where cacao trees were grown by the Maya, and where many similar ceramic artifacts featuring representations of this important crop have been discovered by archeologists.

See also **Tribute being Paid** (pages 174 to 179).

Cacao beans were commonly used as a form of currency by the Maya, as well as by other Mesoamerican peoples. The heap of piled-up cacao beans from which the woman appears to have emerged would have represented enormous riches at the time that this artifact was modeled.

The size of the ear adornments that the woman portrayed on the censer lid is wearing indicates that she should be regarded as a person of high status, and consequently that the cacao beans that surround her have equal importance, or value, within Maya society.

Numerous cacao beans adorn the woman's gown.

A pair of large cacao pods can be seen within the pot that the woman is holding.

Funerary Mask

AD c.200–600

Jade, mother of pearl, and pyrite, from Tikal, Petén, Guatemala, Museo Nacional de Arqueología y Etnología, Guatemala City, Guatemala

The exquisitely crafted jade face mask that was excavated from Burial 160 in the ruined ancient Maya city of Tikal was never intended to see the light of day again after its interment well over a thousand years ago. For it was made specifically to provide a "face" for the Maya dignitary with whose body it was buried once death had first ravaged, and had then finally obliterated, his own features. Considering it from a twenty-first-century viewpoint, we can therefore see that the mask had a superficial, cosmetic function. Those who commissioned and created it had a far more profound purpose in mind, however, for they believed that it would enable its wearer to retain, and project, his identity in perpetuity.

Such naturalistic details as the human-shaped eyes suggest that this was a portrait mask that recreated the deceased's appearance in life, at least as far as the desire to idealize the features of the honored dead and the materials used allowed. (And jade, or jadeite, is an extremely hard substance, making it difficult to shape and carve—particularly in the absence of metal tools—so that the outstanding workmanship that is evident in this mask is testimony to the extraordinary skill of its creator.) The Maya believed that by symbolically preserving his facial appearance, the mask would ensure that its wearer's identity and importance were proclaimed as he undertook the journey through the trials of the underworld that began at his burial. And when he ultimately emerged from the darkness and achieved spiritual reincarnation—as symbolized by the sun's daily regeneration at dawn—the mask again signified his new afterlife identity as the now immortal ancestor of his earthly descendants. The mask thus symbolizes the fusion of the wearer's physical, mortal self (as represented by the human skull behind it) and his spiritual, immortal self (as signified by the idealized mask itself).

Details of the actual identity and life of the man behind the mask are uncertain. Yet because the Maya valued jade above any other natural treasure (including gold), and because the artisan who transformed a handful of rough jade nuggets into the polished work of art that was recovered from Burial 160 was clearly a master craftsman, his mask tells us that the man whose body was entombed with it was a person of high rank in Maya society—someone of noble or royal birth, and maybe even a ruler of Tikal.

See also **Polychrome Two-part Effigy Vessel** (pages 109 to 110).

A headdress featuring delicate decorative and symbolic chasing surmounts the mask's facial section, signaling the wearer's identity and importance.

It is possible that the hooked protuberance overhanging the equally finely modeled human nose below represents the beak of a quetzal bird (called *k'uk'* in the Mayan language). So magnificent is the male quetzal's plumage that it came to be associated with the Maya concept of kingship.

Indeed, some Mayanists have linked the wearer of this funerary mask with K'uk' Ahau— Lord Quetzal—the eighteenth king of Tikal, who was buried, it is thought, in around AD 527.

Mother of pearl has been inlaid within a pair of almond-shaped apertures to represent the whites of the eyes, making a striking contrast to the green of the jade.

Like other shells, mother of pearl would have been collected from a coastal location before being transported inland to be traded.

The large circles at the base of the mask's ear sections replicate the ear spools, or ear flares, with which well-to-do Maya adorned themselves in life. And the larger such pieces of jewelry, the higher the wearer's social status.

The choice of jade for this burial mask was not only dictated by the stone's hardness, durability, relative rarity, and consequent costliness.

Indeed, it held great symbolic significance for the Maya, its greenish-blue color (and an apple-green hue was most highly prized) associating it variously with water, healthy young maize shoots, and the sky, and therefore causing it to denote fertility, life, growth, and regeneration. The jade from which Maya artifacts were formed came from streams and rivers in the southern Maya highlands.

Quiché Burial or Cache Urn Lid

AD 650–850

Earthenware, Museum of Fine Arts, Boston, Massachusetts

The Late Classic Quiché burial or cache urn pictured here, which was discovered in Guatemala's southern highlands, is in such good condition that the colors with which it was originally painted are still evident. Its details have aided scholars' understanding of how the ancient Maya perceived death and the afterlife. Although it is not certain exactly what purpose this earthenware artifact was intended to serve, it almost certainly had a ritual funerary function related to the making of offerings to the gods and to deified ancestors.

The most significant part of the vessel is the lid. The open mouth of a monstrous creature that can be seen here may represent the entrance to the underworld, or *xibalba* ("place of fright"). As related in the Quiché Maya's sacred book the *Popol Vuh*, this was where the death gods who inhabited *xibalba* summoned first Hun Hunahpu, or the Maize God (also known as God E), and later his sons, the Hero Twins. Hun Hunahpu was decapitated and his body buried beneath a *xibalban* ballcourt, but was subsequently resurrected with the help of his sons, this rebirth often being depicted as the Maize God emerging from a crack in a turtle's carapace (see pages 95 to 97). This cycle is mirrored by the way maize kernels planted in the earth germinate, break the soil's surface, and later grow into tall, corncob-bearing plants each year. Not only did the Maize God symbolize essential sustenance (maize being the staple food of the Maya) and therefore life, as well as the principle of regeneration, but he may furthermore have been considered a divine father figure, for the Maya believed that the first humans had been modeled by the gods from a dough made from yellow and white ears of maize (*Zea mays*). The Maya therefore hoped that they, like the Maize God, whose physical appearance they strove to emulate, would survive the horrors of *xibalba* after they had died, after which they would be born again into the afterlife.

See also **"The Creator of the World"** (pages 95 to 97).

The ripe yellow corncobs held by the figure sitting at the apex of the urn's lid indicate that he is the Maize God.

His enormous headdress and prominent ear flares and necklace are signs of his importance, while the blue–green color with which his jewelry has been painted was intended to signify jade, a stone that the Maya associated with water, young maize plants, and fertility, and thus with the life force (see page 188).

Being their staple crop, maize was of the utmost importance to the Maya, who furthermore believed that their earliest ancestors had been formed from maize dough. Indeed, in many depictions of both the Maize God and élite Maya males, it is clear that their long, tapering facial shape, running from the nose through the forehead to the crown of the head, resembles the shape of a corncob.

This effect may have been conveyed through the use of artistic license, but, in the case of Maya men, may also have been achieved in real life through constant pressure being applied to the soft bones of their skulls in babyhood in order to reshape them.

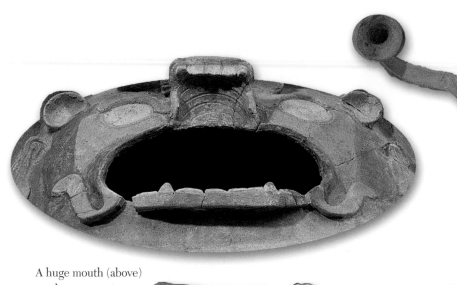

A huge mouth (above) can be seen gaping beneath the cross-legged Maize God. An upturned snout flanked by a pair of round eyes, along with a row of teeth ranged along its lower jaw and bounded by a barbel on each side, together point to a monstrous creature whose maw may signify a portal from this world to *xibalba*, the underworld. In the context of this particular artifact, its purpose may have been to provide easy access to the urn's interior, perhaps so that offerings could be inserted within it, thereby being symbolically sent to a recipient in the underworld, divine realm, or afterlife, such as a deified ancestor.

The circular eyes, tooth-punctuated upper jaw, and long, pointed snout of another fantastic creature is visible at the top of the lower portion of the urn (detail above). This may be a representation of the "Xoc monster," a saurian or sharklike being (see also page 139).

His goggling "god-eyes," which feature hooked internal lines, are the main clue that this face (below) belongs to a deity.

That the face represented at the center of the urn's lower section should be regarded as emerging from the jaws of a monstrous being is emphasized by the line of teeth that can be seen beneath its chin, which suggest the creature's bottom jaw. This part of the vessel may therefore be interpreted as signifying a supernatural domain, which can be entered and exited through the monster's mouth.

Funerary Urn with Feline Lid   AD 550–950

Earthenware with polychrome painting, Museum of Fine Arts, Houston, Texas

Mayanists believe that as well as being utilized as incense-burners (censers, or incensarios), many of the large earthenware vessels unearthed in Guatemala by archeologists may have held the bones of the dead, placed there once their flesh had decomposed and their bodies had been reduced to skeletons. And certainly, with its monstrous symbolic portal and divine face, the lower section of the painted earthenware urn shown at right can be read as representing the underworld domain of the dead. The Quiché Maya equated this with *xibalba*, the "place of fright" where Hun Hunahpu died at the hands of the death gods, as related in the *Popol Vuh*, who were in turn defeated by his sons the Hero Twins (see pages 190 to 192). It seems that the Maya believed that they, too, were destined to descend to the underworld after their deaths, where they would be required to survive all manner of trials and tribulations before they, like the Hero Twins, could rise again to take their places in the heavenly realm.

The jaguar that appears to be guarding this Quiché Maya funerary urn from its vantage point at the top of the vessel's lid was no doubt meant to serve a protective purpose, that is, to act as a symbolic deterrent should anyone, or anything, approach with the intention of damaging the urn's contents. For as well as being feared and respected on account of its predatory strength, bravery, and ferocity, the nocturnal jaguar (*Panthera onca*) was associated in the Maya mind with darkness, and thus with death and the underworld—indeed, the sun god was thought to travel though *xibalba* at night in the form of the Jaguar God of the Underworld (see pages 116 to 118). This jaguar may furthermore represent the *uay* (or *way*) of the person whose remains once lay within the urn, this being an animal spirit companion or alter ego into which shape-shifting shamans and Maya kings could supposedly transform themselves when in a deep trance, enabling them to communicate directly with the supernatural realm.

See also **Quiché Burial or Cache Urn Lid** (pages 190 to 192).

With its rounded ears, glaring eyes, blunt nose, bared teeth, and sharp claws, this feline form represents a jaguar, a beast that the Maya both feared and revered, and that they linked with the night and the underworld. Shamans were also thought to be able to transform themselves into jaguars.

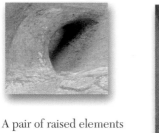

A pair of raised elements on the lid were probably included to serve as handles.

A row of white fangs and incisor teeth line the ridged snout of a monstrous creature that also possesses a pair of round eyes, within which hooked lines are visible. This supernatural being may represent the "earth monster" whose yawning mouth (which also features in sacred Maya architecture) was thought by the Maya to provide access to the underworld.

Emerging as it apparently is from the jaws of the "earth monster," it seems that this face (left) should be interpreted as belonging to an underworld deity. There is certainly nothing human about its circular eyes, whose internal, crooklike motifs echo those of the fantastic being above it. Neither are the barbels that snake out of the corners of its mouth human features. These barbels may reflect the belief that *xibalba* was a watery realm, and also the *Popol Vuh*'s description of the Hero Twins transforming themselves into people–fish while in *xibalba*. In Maya art, they may be depicted in this form as catfish, complete with barbels.

Incense-burner from Funerary Urn from Tapijulapa, Tabasco

Date unknown

Terra cotta, Museo Regional de Antropologia Carlos Pellicer Cámara, Tabasco, Villahermosa, Mexico

Like another funerary urn, or vessel for the ritual burning of incense, pictured in this book (see pages 116 to 118), the Maya artifact shown opposite was discovered in a cave in southern Tabasco, Mexico. The Maya considered caves to be entrances to *xibalba*, the "place of fright," or underworld, to which the newly deceased were obliged to descend, it was thought, once they had departed this life. In so doing, the Maya believed that they were following in the footsteps of Hun Hunahpu and the Hero Twins, and that on their arrival there they would face numerous ordeals devised by the terrible death gods, as described in the sacred book the *Popol Vuh* (see pages 53 to 55). And like the incense-burner discussed on pages 116 to 118), which depicts the Jaguar God of the Underworld, the imagery projected by the ceramic incensario seen here is explicitly linked to death and *xibalba*.

Although it is not certain whether the figure that resembles a human male—albeit with a monstrous nose—portrayed at the center of the incensario is meant to be a priest or an underworld deity, such as a death god, Mayanists have concluded that the mask that forms the object's base represents a bat. The Maya regarded these winged mammals—creatures of the night that roost in caves—as dangerous and even potentially deadly, and, indeed, the *Popol Vuh* relates that when the Hero Twins were in *xibalba*, they hid inside their blowguns while in the House of Bats to escape the murderous attacks of its inhabitants: enormous bats with flint blades for snouts. When Hunahpu peeked out of his blowgun to see whether the coast was clear, Zotz, or Camazotz, the killer bat, swooped down and cut off his head, which the death gods then used as the ball in a ballgame (see pages 47 to 49). It may have been observing bats snatching fruit from trees in mid-flight that led the Maya to associate them with the predilection for decapitation demonstrated by Zotz.

See also **Incense-burner from Funerary Urn Depicting the Jaguar God of the Underworld** (pages 116 to 118).

His fleshless, almost skull-like face and staring eyes give the priest or death god an extremely aged—if not cadaverous—appearance. His nose looks like an animal's snout, and yet he wears a large pair of ear flares, a distinctly human status symbol.

Traces of the vivid blue pigment with which the incensario was originally painted still survive.

Although they are not obviously discernible here, among the Maya death symbols that often feature on underworld-related artifacts are elements of the glyphs denoting Venus (*ek'*) and darkness (*akab* or *akbal*), as well as a curved line between two dots that together look rather like the modern percentage sign (%).

The round beads that the central figure wears around his neck may, like many similar representations of underworld characters, represent plucked-out eyeballs extracted from the bodies of the dead.

A diminutive face is visible among the incense-burner's decorative elements.

The rectangular object—maybe an apron—that is decorated with a cross and four dots has, it is thought, cosmic significance, in that it may signify a celestial conjunction or the four cardinal directions or quarters of the cosmos.

Its circular, beady eyes, wide snout, and the two fangs that protrude from either side of it have led scholars to identify the mask on which the central figure is seated (main picture, above) as representing a

bat. To the Maya bats were associated with darkness, decapitation, and death. In addition, because bats seem to flit between this world and the underworld via caves, it is likely that this bat also represents a portal to, or access to, *xibalba*.

EPILOGUE TO THE MAYA

The Aztec Sun Stone AD 1479

Basalt, Museo Nacional de Arquelogia, Mexico City, Mexico

Just as there are a number of similarities between the Maya and Aztec (Mexica) creation myths, so there is a significant overlap in the way in which both Mesoamerican cultures measured time. Sadly, no comparable Maya equivalent to the Aztec Sun Stone, or Calendar Stone, has yet come to light, but then many of the concepts symbolically conveyed by this huge, carved basalt artifact would have been familiar to the Maya mind. Accidentally hit upon in 1790, by workers digging beneath a plaza in Mexico City, the Aztec Sun Stone—whose diameter is 12 feet—may look rather drab in the photograph here, but would have been brought to vibrant life by the bright colors in which it was originally painted. As its alternative names suggest, aspects of two major themes are expressed by its incised images and glyphs: the "five suns" of creation, and the calendars with which the Aztec (and Maya) regulated time.

At the center of the Sun Stone are five symbols representing the four ages, or "suns," that the Aztec believed the world had experienced in the past, along with the present (and, it is said, final) one. The first sun was Nahui Ocelotl (or 4 Jaguar), whose presiding god was Tezcatlipoca, and whose inhabitants' fate was being devoured by jaguars. The second sun was Nahui Ehecatl (4 Wind), whose deity was Ehecatl–Quetzalcoatl, and whose inhabitants were swept away by the wind. Nahui Quiahuitl (4 Rain) was the name of the third sun, which was ruled by Tlaloc before being annihilated by fiery rain. The fourth sun was Nahui Atl (4 Water), whose deity was the goddess Chalchiuhtlicue, and which was obliterated by a great flood. The present, fifth sun, Nahui Ollin (4 Movement), was created at Teotihuacan after the world was shaped by the dismemberment of the earth deity Tlaltecuhtli and the lowly god Nanahuatzin sacrificed himself to become the sun god Tonatiuh. The *Popol Vuh*, the Quiché Maya's sacred account, similarly tells of successive ages, focusing on the consecutive creation of the animals, a mud person, effigies of carved wood and rushes, and finally of humans formed from maize dough.

Common to both the Maya and the Aztec were also the ritual 260-day calendar (which the Maya called the *tzolkin*, and the Aztec, the *tonalpohualli*), with its twenty day names and thirteen day numbers, and the civil 365-day calendar—the Maya *haab* and the Aztec *xiuhpohualli*—which comprised eighteen months consisting of twenty days, plus five days at the end. Operating in conjunction, the *tzolkin/tonalpohualli* and *haab/xiuhpohualli* created the Calendar Round, a 52-year cycle.

Symbolic details alluding to all of these concepts of time can be seen within the Aztec Sun Stone.

See also **Cylindrical Vases Depicting Ballplayers and a Ballgame** (pages 50 to 60).

This symbol represents the Aztec year 13 Acatl (or 13 Reed), comprising as it does thirteen dotted circles ranged around the glyph representing the *acatl* ("reed") day sign of the Aztec *tonalpohualli*, which, as the thirteenth in the series of twenty day names, corresponds to *ben* ("green maize") in the Maya *tzolkin*. Scholars think that 13 Reed may denote the year in which the Sun Stone was completed: AD 1479.

The identical, five-element motifs that fill the fourth circle from the center (detail above) are believed to signify five-day weeks, of which there are 52 in a 260-day-long period.

The eight pointed, arrowlike symbols that surround the third circle from the center signify sunrays (above), and are positioned at the cardinal and ordinal points, with north, east, south, and west being indicated by the larger arrows.

The outline of the various elements within the second circle form the shape of the glyph that symbolizes *ollin* (meaning "movement," with earthquake connotations), the seventeenth day sign in the Aztec 260-day calendar, whose Maya equivalent was *caban* ("earth").

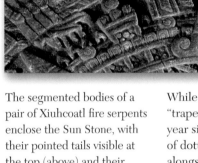

The segmented bodies of a pair of Xiuhcoatl fire serpents enclose the Sun Stone, with their pointed tails visible at the top (above) and their heads—jaws wide open, each disgorging a deity—facing one another at the bottom (below). A being associated with the solar year, the symbols within each segment of the Xiuhcoatl fire serpent's body look like flames.

While its tail resembles the "trapeze-and-ray" Aztec year sign, the double row of dotted circles and lines alongside it signifies dry grass (a symbol of solar heat), and the four "knotted" strips a little farther down along the body represent the paper that was used in Aztec (and Maya) bloodletting and offering rituals.

The five circles that can be seen within the ring of twenty day signs denote the five "empty" days (*nemontemi*) at the end of each solar year (falling at the end of a series of eighteen twenty-day months), which were considered inauspicious.

The Maya equivalent "vague-year" solar calendar, the *haab*, was similarly divided into eighteen months of twenty days, with a five-day *uayeb* period concluding the 365-day cycle (see also pages 76 to 77).

Each of the twenty segments into which the third circle from the center has been divided represents one of the day signs of the *tonalpohualli*, the Aztec 260-day calendar. *Ollin* ("movement"), for example, the seventeenth in the series, can be seen at about the 2 o'clock position.

This symbol (above) represents the third sun, Nahui Quiahuitl (4 Rain). *Quiahuitl*, the nineteenth day name of the Aztec 260-day calendar, signifies "rain," the corresponding Maya day name, *cauac*, varying slightly in meaning "storm."

The second sun, Nahui Ehecatl (4 Wind), is symbolized to the left of a central sunray. According to the 260-day calendar known as *tonalpohualli* by the Aztecs (and the *tzolkin* by the Maya), the second day name was called either *ehecatl* (by the Aztecs) or *ik'* (by the Maya), although the meaning was the same: "wind."

A jaguar represents the first sun, Nahui Ocelotl (4 Jaguar). *Ocelotl* was the fourteenth day sign of the Aztec 260-day calendar, corresponding to the Maya *ix*, both denoting "jaguar."

Claws clutching human hearts—the ultimate sacrificial offering to the gods—have been inscribed to the left and right of the central image. The claws should probably be envisaged as belonging to Tonatiuh, with the hearts signifying the energy source required to sustain him, and thus also the age of the fifth sun.

It was said that the sun god Tonatiuh had refused to move across the sky until the gods had sacrificed themselves to him and had offered him their hearts. This they did, and in Aztec belief, humans must continue to do the same, in order to ensure that the sun rises in the east each day.

The face portrayed at the centre of the stone is thought most likely to be that of Tonatiuh, the god of the sun and of the east who presides over the current era (alternatively, some scholars believe it to belong to the earth deity Tlaltecuhtli). His protruding tongue has been interpreted as representing a sacrificial knife fashioned from either flint or obsidian. He is surrounded by representations of the four previous suns.

Nahui Atl (4 Water), the fourth sun, is represented by this symbol. *Atl* ("water") was the ninth day name in the Aztec *tonalpohualli*, and the equivalent of the Maya *muluc*, similarly meaning "water" (or else "jade").

INDEX

BIBLIOGRAPHY

Baudez, Claude, & Picasso, Sydney, *Lost Cities of the Maya*, Thames & Hudson Ltd., London, 1992.

Christenson, Allen J., *Popol Vuh: The Sacred Book of the Maya*, O Books, Alresford, Hants, 2003.

Coe, Michael, Snow, Dean, & Benson, Elizabeth, *Atlas of Ancient America*, Equinox (Oxford) Ltd., Oxford, 1986.

Coe, Michael D., & Van Stone, Mark, *Reading the Maya Glyphs*, Thames & Hudson Ltd., London, 2001.

Fagan, Brian, *Elusive Treasures: The Story of Early Archaeologists in the Americas*, Book Club Associates, 1978.

Freidel, David, Schele, Linda, & Parker, Joy, *Maya Cosmos: Three Thousand Years on the Shaman's Path*, William Morrow and Company, Inc., New York, 1993.

Gates, William, *Outline Dictionary of Maya Glyphs and Glyph Studies*, Kessinger Publishing, Breinigsville, PA, 2010.

Hagen, Victor von, *Search for the Maya: The Story of Stephens & Catherwood*, Book Club Associates, London, 1973.

Landa, Friar Diego de, *Yucatan Before and After the Conquest*, Dover Publications, Inc., New York, 1978.

Laughton, Timothy, *The Maya: Life, Myth and Art*, Duncan Baird Publishers, London, 1998.

Longhena, Maria, *Ancient Mexico: History and Culture of the Maya, Aztecs and Other Pre-Columbian Populations*, White Star Publishers, Vercelli, 2005.

Miller, Mary Ellen, *Maya Art and Architecture*, Thames & Hudson Ltd., London, 1999.

Miller, Mary, & Taube, Karl, *The Gods and Symbols of Ancient Mexico and the Maya: An Illustrated Dictionary of Mesoamerican Religion*, Thames and Hudson Ltd., London, 1993.

Phillips, Charles, *The Art & Architecture of the Aztec & Maya*, Anness Publishing Ltd., London, 2007.

Phillips, Charles, *The Everyday Life of the Aztec & Maya*, Anness Publishing Ltd., London, 2007.

Stierlin, Henri, *The Art of the Maya*, Benedikt Taschen Verlag GmbH, Köln, 1994.

Stray, Geoff, *The Mayan and Other Ancient Calendars*, Wooden Books Ltd., Glastonbury, 2007.

Taube, Karl, *Aztec & Maya Myths*, The British Museum Press, London, 1993.

Websites
Authentic Maya: http://www.authenticmaya.com/

The Copan National Park: http://www.copanpark.com/

The Corpus of Maya Hieroglyphic Inscriptions (The Peabody Museum of Archaeology and Ethnology): http://140.247.102.177/CMHI/

Foundation for the Advancement of Mesoamerican Studies, Inc.: http://www.famsi.org/

MayaRuins.com: http://mayaruins.com/

Mesoweb: http://www.mesoweb.com/

National Geographic, Maya special issue: http://ngm.nationalgeographic.com/2008/08/maya-issue/table-of-contents

The Wired Humanities Project's Virtual Mesoamerican Archive: http://vma.uoregon.edu/

ACKNOWLEDGMENTS

The publisher would like to thank the following people for their assistance in the preparation of this book: Sara Hunt, editor; Deborah White, art editor/designer; Sara Myers, editorial assistant and indexer; Chloe van Grieken, illustrator and graphic design assistant; Barbara Kerr, Martha Lineham, and Joel Skidmore for their help with images; and the individuals and institutions who gave permission for illustrations to be reproduced here, as listed below by page number. (Note that the institutions listed in the location information on the featured plates have in most cases been represented by the Bridgeman Art Library.) Every effort has been made to credit images and list locations accurately; we apologise if any errors have occurred, and will endeavor to correct these in future editions if notified of queries.

The Bridgeman Art Library: 1 (except far left), 2, 3, 4, 5 (except bottom), 42–43 (all), 45–49 (all), 72–74 (all), 75 (top left), 78–81 (all), 92–121 (all), 132–167 (all), 180–201 (all), 208; **Simon Burchell:** 84 (right); **DinkY2K:** 88–89; **Foundation for the Advancement of Mesoamerican Studies, Inc.:** 1 (far left), 5 (bottom), 6, 10 (left), 32, 35 (all), 37 (both), 39 (all), 40–41, 61–71 (all), 75 (all except top left), 76–77 (all), 86 (both), 87 (all except bottom right); **Luis García:** 84 (left); **Tato Grasso:** 122; © **Chloe van Grieken** (maps, art and illustration): 14, 23, 40–41, 44; © **2010 Jupiter images:** 7, 8–9, 10 (right), 11, 12, 13, 15, 16, 17 (right), 18, 20, 21, 22, 24 (bottom), 25 (both), 26, 27, 28 (both), 29 (both), 30 (both), 31, 33, 36, 38, 82, 83, 85, 87 (bottom right), 88 (top), 89 (top), 90, 91, 123, 125 (bottom), 127 (bottom), 128–131 (all); **E. Kehnel:** 24 (top); © **Justin Kerr:** rollout photographs K638, K1209, K1288, K1728: pages 50–60 (all) and 168–179 (all); **Pgbk87:** 125 (top); © **Dr. Merle Robertson:** pages 42–43, 45–46; © **2004 Jacob Rus:** 124, 126; **A. H. Vega:** 34; © **Deborah White:** 127 (top); **C. Wright:** 17 (left).